MW00344503

Beat Poetry

Larry Beckett

A Beatdom Books Publication

Published by Beatdom Books

Copyright © 2012 by Larry Beckett
Cover photographs by Laura Fletcher
Cover design by Susannah Beckett

All rights reserved. No part of this book may be reproduced in any form or by any electronic or mechanical means including information storage and retrieval systems, without permission in writing from the author. The only exception is by a reviewer, who may quote short excerpts in a review.

Permissions information on p. 148.

View the publisher's website:
www.books.beatdom.com

Printed in the United Kingdom
First Print Edition
ISBN 978-0-9569525-3-0

Contents

Intro

"Paleface and redskin" is how Philip Rahv laid it down in a 1939 issue of the Kenyon Review: the poles of American literature, magnetic repulsion between the values of order and rebellion, form and spontaneity, thought and passion. Hawthorne in his dark house and Whitman on the open road. Writers are one or the other and, as Rahv goes on to say, "no love is lost between them."

This divide was just as great that night in San Francisco, October 1955, in the Six Gallery, converted from an automobile repair shop, when Allen Ginsberg stood on the plywood stage backed by black walls and recited "Howl" Part I. In the audience the wine jug was circling, Jack Kerouac was shouting "Go!", Gary Snyder was standing by with myths and texts, as Lawrence Ferlinghetti listened, with his press ready at City Lights.

That night the San Francisco Renaissance was born, a renaissance of poetry: Lawrence Ferlinghetti's lyrical cityscapes, Jack Kerouac's blues and haikus, Allen Ginsberg's saxophone prophecies, Gregory Corso's obsessive odes, John Wieners' true confessions, Michael McClure's physical hymns, Philip

Lamantia's surreal passions, Gary Snyder's work songs, Philip Whalen's loose sutras, Lew Welch's hermit visions, David Meltzer's improvisations and discoveries, and Bob Kaufman's jazz meditations.

That the renaissance opened at a poetry reading is a sign: in Beat poetry you hear the language of the street, coming back; poems are "oral messages," not to be learned, but lived. There's a reconnection to voice, in a stream of readings: Ginsberg at the Town Hall Theatre, Corso at the San Francisco Poetry Center, Ferlinghetti and Meltzer with a quintet at The Cellar, Kerouac and Lamantia over piano at the Brata Art Gallery, Wieners at The Place, Kaufman at the Co-Existence Bagel Shop, McClure at Fugazi Hall, Welch at International Music Hall.

But the paleface at the critical typewriter has closed his window on the songs of the redskin outside. From the presses of the academy come only Beat biographies, sociologies, encyclopedias, interviews, photographs. . .

This is the missing book, child of the marriage of the skins, ready to trace the roots and branches of the poetry of those streets.

Theme

Let's Shout
  Our Poems
  In San Francisco Streets
    —Jack Kerouac to Allen Ginsberg[10]

In the last line of "Howl," "in my dreams you walk dripping from a sea-journey on the highway across America in tears to the door of my cottage in the Western night," Ginsberg is remembering that strange alchemy, when the beat down eastern writers—Lowell's Jack Kerouac, Newark's Allen Ginsberg, New York's Gregory Corso—went on the road to the west, and with the beatific San Francisco poets—Lawrence Ferlinghetti, Michael McClure, Philip Lamantia—joined by the eastern Bob Kaufman, David Meltzer, John Wieners, and the northern Zen lunacy poets—Gary Snyder, Philip Whalen, Lew Welch— opened a renaissance.

This chronology's by date of publication or composition.

1950   Lawrence Ferlinghetti arrives in San Francisco and
             lives at the Chateau Bleu, 1901 Jackson Street.
             Gary Snyder, Philip Whalen, and Lew Welch room
             together, 2121 Lambert Street, Portland.

1951   Jack Kerouac writes *On the Road* on a scroll in April
             at 454 West Twentieth Street, New York.

1952   Jack Kerouac arrives in January and finishes revising
             On the Road in Neal and Carolyn Cassady's attic, 29
             Russell Street.
             Gary Snyder and Philip Whalen arrive in September
             and room in an apartment at 1201 Montgomery
             Street.

1953   Lawrence Ferlinghetti writes *Pictures of the gone
             world*, 339 Chestnut Street, Apt. 20.
             In June, Lawrence Ferlinghetti and Peter Martin
             open City Lights Bookstore, 261 Columbus Avenue.

1954   Jack Kerouac writes *San Francisco Blues* in April at
             the Cameo Hotel, 389 Third Street.
             Bob Kaufman arrives in June; Allen Ginsberg
             arrives and stays the night in the Geary Hotel, 610
             Geary Street.
             Allen Ginsberg lives in Apt. 5 at 755 Pine Street in
             August, where he sees Moloch out the window: the
             upper stories of the Sir Francis Drake Hotel, 450
             Powell Street.
             Michael McClure arrives in December.

1955   *Reality Sandwiches* (1953-55), Allen Ginsberg:
             unpublished
             The Vestal Lady on Brattle and Other Poems,
             Gregory Corso: Richard Brukenfeld
             Jack Kerouac writes *Mexico City Blues* in August in
             Mexico City,

Allen Ginsberg writes "Howl" Part I, 1010
Montgomery Street, and Gary Snyder writes *Riprap*,
2919 Hillegass Street, Berkeley.
Pictures of the gone world, Lawrence Ferlinghetti:
City Lights
Allen Ginsberg writes "Howl" Part II and III in
September in a cottage behind 1624 Milvia Street,
Berkeley; Philip Whalen rooms with him.
6 Poets at 6 Gallery, in October: introduced by
Kenneth Rexroth, Allen Ginsberg reads "Howl" Part
I, with Philip Lamantia, Michael McClure, Philip
Whalen, Gary Snyder, with Jack Kerouac and
Lawrence Ferlinghetti in the audience, at 3119
Fillmore Street.

1956   The 6 Poets at 6 Gallery is repeated in March at
Town Hall Theatre, Shattuck Avenue and Stuart
Street, Berkeley; Allen Ginsberg reads the complete
"Howl."
Book of Blues, Jack Kerouac: unpublished
Siesta in Xbalba and Return to the States, Allen
Ginsberg: mimeograph
Passage, Michael McClure: Jonathan Williams
Gary Snyder writes *Myths & Texts* in a cabin at 348
Montford Avenue, Mill Valley.
Gregory Corso arrives in August.
Allen Ginsberg finishes revising "Howl" in October.
Howl and Other Poems, Allen Ginsberg: City
Lights
Lawrence Ferlinghetti writes *A Coney Island of the
Mind*, 339 Chestnut Street, Apt. 20.
Gregory Corso recites poetry at The San Francisco
Poetry Center, 1600 Holloway.
David Meltzer arrives and lives in an apartment at
1514 Larkin Street.

1957   *Evergreen Review: Number 2. The San Francisco*

Scene, edited by Donald Allen

Lawrence Ferlinghetti and David Meltzer recite poetry to jazz in March at The Cellar, 576 Green Street.

Poems, David Meltzer: privately printed by Donald & Alice Schenker

Gregory Corso writes first version of *Bomb* in October in Paris.

John Wieners arrives in October.

John Wieners recites poetry for Blabbermouth Night, at The Place, 1546 Grant Avenue.

1958   John Wieners writes *The Hotel Wentley Poems*, 1214 Polk Street.

Book of Haikus, Jack Kerouac: unpublished

Gasoline, Gregory Corso: City Lights

Bomb, Gregory Corso: City Lights broadside

A Coney Island of the Mind, Lawrence Ferlinghetti: New Directions

Gary Snyder lives at the East-West house, 2273 California Street, with Lew Welch, and translates *Cold Mountain Poems.*

Cold Mountain Poems, Han Shan, translated by Gary Snyder, in *Evergreen Review: Number 6*

The Hotel Wentley Poems, John Wieners: Auerhahn Press

Michael McClure writes *Hymns to St. Geryon*, Harwood Alley, now Bob Kaufman Alley, and at 707 Scott Street.

Philip Lamantia writes *Ekstasis*, 1045 Russia Street.

David Meltzer writes *Ragas*, 973 Filbert Street.

Bob Kaufman recites poetry at the Co-Existence Bagel Shop, 1398 Grant Avenue.

Poets Follies, with Lawrence Ferlinghetti and Michael McClure, at Fugazi Hall, 678 Green Street.

Peyote Poem, Michael McClure: Semina 3

1959   Allen Ginsberg and Gregory Corso play in the
Robert Frank / Alfred Leslie film *Pull My Daisy*,
based on Act 3 of Jack Kerouac's play, *Beat
Generation*, filmed in New York, narrated by
Kerouac.
Mexico City Blues, Jack Kerouac: Grove Press
The Auerhahn Press, John Wieners, Michael
McClure, Philip Lamantia, Philip Whalen: Auerhahn
Press
For Artaud, Michael McClure: Totem Press
Hymns to St. Geryon and Other Poems, Michael
McClure: Auerhahn Press
Ekstasis, Philip Lamantia: Auerhahn Press
Narcotica, Philip Lamantia: Auerhahn Press
Riprap, Gary Snyder: Origin Press
Self-Portrait from Another Direction, Philip Whalen:
Auerhahn Press
Ragas, David Meltzer: Discovery Books, from the
Discovery Bookstore, 241 Columbus Avenue
Abomunist Manifesto, Bob Kaufman: City Lights
broadside
Second April, Bob Kaufman: City Lights broadside
Lew Welch lives at the East-West house with Jack
Kerouac, and writes *Wobbly Rock*.
Trip Trap, Jack Kerouac, Albert Saijo, Lew Welch:
unpublished
Allen Ginsberg reads "Kaddish" at the Old
Longshoreman's Hall, 150 Golden Gate.
Bob Kaufman is living at the New Riviera Hotel,
615 Union Street.
Beatitude magazine mimeographed in May at the
Bread and Wine Mission, 501 Greenwich Street.
John Wieners reads in June at The San Francisco
Poetry Center.
Philip Whalen writes *Like I Say*, 1624 Milvia Street,
Berkeley.
Mad Monster Mammoth Poets' Reading in August,

with John Wieners, Philip Lamantia, Lawrence Ferlinghetti, Bob Kaufman, Michael McClure, David Meltzer, Philip Whalen, at Garibaldi Hall.

1960   *Reality Sandwiches* (1956-60), Allen Ginsberg: unpublished
Rimbaud, Jack Kerouac: City Lights broadside
The Happy Birthday of Death, Gregory Corso: New Directions
Myths & Texts, Gary Snyder: Totem/Corinth
Memoirs of an Interglacial Age, Philip Whalen: Auerhahn Press
Like I Say, Philip Whalen: Totem/Corinth
Wobbly Rock, Lew Welch: Auerhahn Press
The Clown, David Meltzer: Semina 6
The New American Poetry: 1945-1960, Edited by Donald Allen: Grove Press

1961   *Pull My Daisy*, Jack Kerouac, Allen Ginsberg, Neal Cassady: Grove Press
Empty Mirror: Early Poems, Allen Ginsberg: Totem/ Corinth
Kaddish and Other Poems: 1958-60, Allen Ginsberg: City Lights
Michael McClure writes *Dark Brown*, 2324 Fillmore Street.
The New Book / A Book of Torture, Michael McClure: Grove Press
Dark Brown, Michael McClure: Auerhahn Press
A Casebook on the Beat, Edited by Thomas Parkinson: Crowell

1962   *Destroyed Works*, Philip Lamantia: Auerhahn Press
Hermit Poems, Lew Welch: unpublished
The Way Back, Lew Welch: unpublished

1963 *Reality Sandwiches: 1953-1960*, Allen Ginsberg:
City Lights
The Change: Poems, Allen Ginsberg: Writer's Forum
Poems, Bob Kaufman: unpublished
Mad Monster Mammoth Poets' Reading in
November, with Lew Welch, Allen Ginsberg,
Philip Whalen, Michael McClure, David Meltzer, at
International Music Hall, 2226A Fillmore Street.

Beat Poetry

1st Chorus:

Gone:

Lawrence Ferlinghetti

In Lawrence Ferlinghetti's inaugural address as San Francisco Poet Laureate, October 1998, he said:

> "When I arrived in the City in 1950, I came overland by train and took ferry from the Oakland mole to the Ferry Building. And San Francisco looked like some Mediterranean port—a small white city, with mostly white buildings—a little like Tunis seen from seaward. I thought perhaps it was Atlantis, risen from the sea. I certainly saw North Beach especially as a poetic place, as poetic as some quartiers in Paris, as any place in old Europa, as poetic as any place great poets and painters had found inspiration. And this was the first poem[12] I wrote here. . . a North Beach scene:"[18]

Beat Poetry

Away above a harborful
                              of caulkless houses
among the charley noble chimneypots
                              of a rooftop rigged with clotheslines
    a woman pastes up sails
                              upon the wind
  hanging out her morning sheets
                              with wooden pins
              O lovely mammal
                              her nearly naked breasts
        throw taut shadows
                              when she stretches up
    to hang at last the last of her
                              so white washed sins
      but it is wetly amorous
                              and winds itself about her
          clinging to her skin
                              So caught with arms upraised
      she tosses back her head
                              in voiceless laughter
    and in choiceless gesture then
                              shakes out gold hair

while in the reachless seascape spaces

                    between the blown white shrouds

    stand out the bright steamers

                              to kingdom come

This poem, written in three sentences by a painter, is a word painting of a woman hanging out laundry: beauty in the ordinary, sensuous and sensual. It has a simple, fresh, improvised air. Unlike academic poems of its day, it needs no footnotes, though it might be said that the melodies on the letter *a* in the first line, "Away above a harborful," and the thirteenth, "to hang at last the last of her," echo the last phrases of James Joyce's *Finnegans Wake*, 1939:[19] "A way a lone a last a loved a long the"; "Charley noble" is sailor's jargon for the galley chimney; the tenth line has "breasts" as first printed in *Pictures of the gone world*, and "teats" as reprinted in *A Coney Island of the Mind*, with the two editions concurrent.

Its layout, splashed across the page in left and right lines, reaches toward the visual in a way derived from Stéphane Mallarmé's *A Throw of the Dice (Un coup de des)*, 1897,[20] with its seagoing imagery mirrored in the array of the words, as in this page:

An insinuation   simple

   in the silence   enrolled with irony
                   or
                    the mystery

                          hurled

                          howled

 in some nearby   whirlpool of hilarity and horror

       flutters   about the abyss
                    without strewing it

                     or fleeing

        and out of it cradles the virgin sign

There are other parallels between Ferlinghetti and the French poet. Mallarmé wrote reviews of the local impressionists, including his friends Édouard Manet and Edgar Degas; the pages of *A Throw of the Dice* lean toward representation: wave, ship, constellation. Ferlinghetti wrote reviews of the local abstract expressionists, who rediscovered impressionism, including his acquaintances Mark Rothko and probably Richard Diebenkorn; the pages of *Pictures of the gone world* lean toward abstraction, using positive and negative space.

Like Mallarmé, in the words of Barry Silesky's *Ferlinghetti: the Artist in His Time*, "Ferlinghetti wanted to use the page as a canvas. Rather than being restricted to the left margin, these poems were designed to use the whole page. . . the way painters spread paint."[21] Poetry happens not only in the language, but between the lines, in the white space.

In his introduction to *A Throw of the Dice*, Mallarmé talks about the effect of that space on the sound: "This copied distance, which mentally separates words or groups of words from one another, has the literary advantage. . . of seeming to speed up and slow down the movement, of scanning it. . ."[20] So, if Ferlinghetti's poem were left-justified and the left and right lines joined and punctuated, the run-on lines would read as andante:

> Away above a harborful of caulkless houses,
> among the charley noble chimneypots of a rooftop
>   rigged with clotheslines,
> a woman pastes up sails upon the wind,

but ranged as it is and unpunctuated, it's adagio:

> Away above a harborful
>   of caulkless houses
> among the charley noble chimneypots
>   of a rooftop rigged with clotheslines
>   a woman pastes up sails
>   upon the wind

There is a loose form: a left-side line may begin anywhere as long as it's toward the left of center. This is followed by a right-side line, which may begin anywhere as long as it's toward the right. Each side line can have between four and nine syllables; the break can come anywhere, and the rhythm is rising, with variation. This form gives an air of freedom, but retains music. The left and right pairs can make common blank verse:

> a woman pastes up sails upon the wind
>
> . . .
>
> she tosses back her head in voiceless laughter

There's an easygoing alliteration: "harborful / houses, charley / chimneypots, rooftop / rigged, nearly / naked." The vertical space between the lines increases in the last four and, read as longer silences, create emphasis by ritenuto.

"Harborful" is the first in a series of quiet coinings, on the model of "voiceless": "caulkless / choiceless / reachless"; these give the poem an experimental tone, underlined by the last phrase, pure slang: "kingdom come." The harbor's boats are metonymically named "caulkless houses," and the sheets being hung, "sails" and "sins," but beyond that there are no figures. Mallarmé uses the concrete form to make ambiguous syntax, non-linear statement, and symbols, while Ferlinghetti is direct but evocative.

He looks out the window, not at nature but at the city: at the harbor, up to a roof, at the steamships. This is natural for Ferlinghetti, whose thesis at the Sorbonne in Paris was "The City as a Symbol in Modern Poetry: In Search of a Metropolitan Tradition." It was Charles Baudelaire who made poetry able to include the city; his *Flowers of Evil*, 1865, was the first book of poetry Ferlinghetti read. This is from "The Swan":[22]

> Some echo fertilized my magpie mind,
> as I was crossing the new Carrousel.
> Old Paris is done for. (Our cities find
> new faces sooner than the heart.) Its shell

was all I noticed, when I strolled beneath
its barracks, heaps of roughed-out capitals,
stray apple carts, troughs, greening horses' teeth,
commercial gypsies clinking in their stalls.

A strolling circus had laid out its tent,
where I was dragging home through the dawn's red;
labor was rising, and a sprinkler spread
a hurricane to lay the sediment.

I saw a swan that had escaped its cage,
and struck its dry wings on the cobbled street,
and drenched the curbing with its fluffy plumage.
Beside a gritty gutter, it dabbed its feet. . .

While writing *Pictures of the gone world*, Ferlinghetti was reading the cultural magazine *City Lights*, where, according to Neeli Cherkovski's *Ferlinghetti: A Biography*, "Robert Duncan, for example, wrote of the need to create poetry out of the street, the need to learn to appreciate the spirit of the city. . ." It was there that Ferlinghetti published the first English translations of the urban poetry of Jacques Prévert, from *Paroles*, 1946:[24]

And the Fête Continues

Standing before the bar
At the stroke of ten
A tall plumber
Dressed for sunday on monday
Sings for himself alone
Sings that it's thursday
That there's no school today
That the war is over
And work too
That life is so beautiful
And the girls so pretty

And staggering by the bar
But guided by his plumb-line
He stops dead before the proprietor
Three peasants will pass and pay you
Then disappears in the sun
Without settling for the drinks
Disappears in the sun all the while singing his song.

This is Ferlinghetti's vein: from the streets, simple, lyrical.

In "Away above a harborful," the poet sees the woman try to transcend her white-washed sins, by washing and hanging up the sheets where she committed them, but they're wetly amorous and wrap themselves around her; she sees she can't escape them, and so accepts them and laughs. But this is all said glancingly; as the poem unfolds, the heart of it is the poet seeing the city—boats, chimneypots, rooftop, clotheslines—and then, in the midst of it, this natural vision: "O lovely mammal."

"O lovely mammal" is a characteristic Beat note: to take a classic rhetorical gesture, and warp it back to the everyday. For example, apostrophe, where the absent or inanimate is addressed as though present and human, as in "O minstrel harp, still must thine accents sleep" from *The Lady of the Lake* by Walter Scott. The "O" sets up expectation of apostrophe and its grandeur, which is turned to anticlimax: "O foot tired in climes so mysterious" from "He is your friend, let him dream" by Jack Kerouac;[43] "O skinny legions run outside" from "Howl" Part III by Allen Ginsberg;[55] "O Spring Bomb / Come with thy gown of dynamite green" from *Bomb* by Gregory Corso.[69] "Mammal" evokes mammaries, and centers on the woman's animal sexuality. This vision is ecstatic, finding heaven on earth in the sexual pun "kingdom come."

Out of French inspirations, Baudelaire's city, Mallarmé's visuals, Prévert's simplicity, Ferlinghetti found a way to make San Francisco poetry. In this poem, everything's open: the window, the boats, the rooftop, her blouse, the wild horizon, as the steamers mysteriously head out for the next world; everything's loose: the sheets, her laughter, her gesture, her hair, this music.

"Away above a harborful" is number 1 in the book *Pictures of the gone world*.[12] The word "Pictures" invokes the visual, and the poems allude to the artists Praxiteles, Brancusi, Sarolla, Picasso. "Gone" has the common meanings departed and hopeless, but these are balanced by meanings in mid-fifties musical slang: great, or fine, as in the Fats Domino song "I'm Gonna Be a Wheel Someday": "I'm gonna be a real gone cat"; and inspired, or ecstatic, as in the Elvis Presley song "Mystery Train": "Let's get real gone for a change."

The word Beat, originally carnival slang used to describe the hard up lives of carnies on the road, was first used by Kerouac in a 1948 conversation with the novelist John Clellon Holmes: "So I guess you might say we're a beat generation." Holmes put it in print, in the 1952 *New York Times Magazine* article, "This Is the Beat Generation".[4] It has a double significance, both originated by Kerouac: first, beat down, and later, beatific—in his words, "beat, meaning down and out but full of intense conviction".[34] The tones and overtones of "gone" mirror it.

The book has twenty-seven poems, numbered as though verses of a single long poem, many with little more compression than ordinary speech; it can be carried in a pocket, and read in less than an hour. The poems trace mortality, love, art, observed in reality, refracted in fantasy, in the cities, Paris, London, New York, San Francisco. Their forms modify the layout to convey the tone. Their ideas run counter to mainstream culture, expressing Ferlinghetti's values as affirmed or extended by the poet and anarchist Kenneth Rexroth, mentor to many, and his circle. They mock intellectuals, conformists, militarists; their heart goes out to lovers, animals, artists.

The book was self-published in 1955. Ferlinghetti had joined with Peter Martin, the editor of *City Lights* magazine, to form the landmark City Lights Bookstore; its publishing house issued broadsides, including *Bomb* by Corso and *Abomunist Manifesto* and *Second April* by Bob Kaufman, and the Pocket Poets series, including his own *Pictures of the gone world*, *Howl and Other Poems* and *Reality Sandwiches* by Ginsberg, *Gasoline* by Corso, *Selected Poems* by Philip Lamantia, and *Scattered Poems* by

Kerouac.

Ferlinghetti's next book is *A Coney Island of the Mind*,[15] its title taken from the dream chapter "Into the Night Life" in Henry Miller's *Black Spring*, 1936; it's dedicated to K., not Kafka's antihero, but Ferlinghetti's wife, nicknamed Kirby. It was published in 1958 by New Directions, who also brought out *The Happy Birthday of Death* by Corso, and *Solitudes Crowded with Loneliness* by Kaufman. It's a composite book, comprising the title section, a section called "Oral Messages", and, to make it long enough to suit the publisher, selections from the first book. This composite quality can be seen in many Beat poetry texts, and shows radically different kinds of poetry in one volume.

The first section is twenty-nine poems continuing in the style of *Pictures*, but more varied and accomplished, ending with a run-on prose poem celebrating love and sex through literature, again including an allusion to the last line of *Finnegans Wake*:[19] "away alone at last and loved." One of them, number 15,[15] is this enduring poem, an ars poetica, in three sentences:

Constantly risking absurdity

     and death

 whenever he performs

    above the heads

      of his audience

 the poet like an acrobat

   climbs on rime

    to a high wire of his own making

and balancing on eyebeams

    above a sea of faces

  paces his way

   to the other side of day

 performing entrechats

    and sleight-of-foot tricks

and other high theatrics

        and all without mistaking

    any thing

        for what it may not be

   For he's the super realist

        who must perforce perceive

    taut truth

        before the taking of each stance or step

in his supposed advance

        toward that still higher perch

where Beauty stands and waits

      with gravity

        to start her death-defying leap

   And he

    a little charleychaplin man

        who may or may not catch

    her fair eternal form

        spreadeagled in the empty air

    of existence

The second section, "Oral Messages," is seven poems introduced by the author as "not written for the printed page" but "spontaneously spoken," like a solo in jazz, "for jazz accompaniment."[15] Inspired by Ginsberg's reading of "Howl" Part I at the 6 Gallery, and invited by Rexroth, Ferlinghetti recited these poems at a club with the Cellar Jazz Quintet. Two of them, "Autobiography" and "Junkman's Obbligato," were recorded in 1957;[14] both *Pictures*[13] and *Coney Island*[16] were recorded complete years later, with music. The oral quality of the poetry is signaled, ironically, by conventional left-justified lines, as in the opening of "Dog",[15] although this sound is slowed down in the last twenty-seven lines by the now familiar array:

> The dog trots freely in the street,
> and sees reality
> and the things he sees
> are bigger than himself
> and the things he sees
> are his reality
> Drunks in doorways
> Moons on trees

He says of these poems that as a result of performances "they are still in a state of change."[15] This suggests that new poetry can occur in reciting it, or because of reciting it. The idea that the text is a basis for improvisation, like a jazz chart, is very experimental, making poetry a process more than an object. The poet is free of the text, and able to reshape it in the next performance. The short free verse lines, typically between four and eight syllables, lend themselves to spontaneous variation. The dog trots freely: freedom is the process, the sound, the message.

In the street: Ferlinghetti's poems appeal not to mind only, but to eye and ear; they're not for virtue only, but for pleasure. He is well aware of how his rejection of classical form and his commitment to visuality and orality distance him from academic poets and critics. In "Notes on Poetry in San Francisco," written at the same time, he says, "The poetry which has been making itself heard here of late is what should be called street poetry. . . It amounts to getting poetry back into the street, where it once was, out of the classroom, out of the speech department, and—in fact—off the printed page. . . I walked through Chinatown recently with a famous academic poet, and he never saw the whole schools of fish gaping on counters, nor heard what they breathed."[17]

The connection to the street is two-way: the sensations, the language, of the street—vital, colloquial, sexual—go into the poem, which is read out loud to the people in the street. Poetry is taken out of the context of learning, and made a part of life.

This doesn't mean turning away from culture, however. The first section of the book alludes directly to Goya, Homer, Pound, Thoreau, Keats, Bosch, Graves, Dante, Chagall, Kafka, Cellini, Picasso, Hopkins, Eliot, Hemingway, Shakespeare, Proust, Barnes, Lorca, Joyce, Tolstoy, Chekhov.

Literary allusion is a primary device in Ferlinghetti's street poetry. In the oral message "Autobiography," for example, there is allusion to author:

> I see they're making Melville
> eat his whale.

to title, as in Marcel Proust, from the book of Genesis:

> Crossed the Jersey Flats
> and seen the Cities of the Plain

and Thomas Wolfe:

> I looked homeward
> and saw no angel.

to character:

> I thought I was Tom Sawyer
> catching crayfish in the Bronx River

and allusion to phrase, which by variation or context is made to be satiric, witty, touching, haunting, and which is so continuous that the poem is a virtual cento. There is old Welsh poetry, as rendered in *The White Goddess*

> I have seen the White Goddess dancing
> in the Rue des Beaux Arts

by Robert Graves, in Taliesin's conundrum:[25]

I have sat in an uneasy chair.

and in "The Song of Amergin," which includes these lines:

> I am a tear of the sun,
> I am fair among flowers,
> I am a boar,
> I am a salmon in a pool,
> I am a lake on a plain,
> I am a hill of poetry,

with the allusions:

> I am a tear of the sun.
> I am a hill
> where poets run.
> . . .
> I am a lake upon a plain.
> I am a word
> in a tree.
> I am a hill of poetry.
> . . .
> For I am a still
> of poetry.

There is Romantic poetry, as in William Wordsworth's "I wandered lonely as a cloud" crossed with David Riesman's sociological study *The Lonely Crowd*:

> I have wandered lonely
> as a crowd.

and George Byron's *Childe Harold's Pilgrimage*:

> I have heard the sound of revelry
> by night.

and John Keats' "La Belle Dame sans Merci:"

> and the Beautiful Dame Without Mercy
> . . .
> and no bird sang.

Victorian poetry, as in Matthew Arnold's "Dover Beach":

> I have seen the educated armies
> on the beach at Dover.

Modernist poetry, as in T. S. Eliot's *Four Quartets*:

> I am a raid
> on the inarticulate

and W. B. Yeats' "Under Ben Bulben," and epitaph, "Horseman, pass by!"

> instructing the horsemen
> to pass.

Modernist prose, as in Thomas Wolfe's *Look Homeward Angel*:

> looking for a stone a leaf
> an unfound door.

and James Joyce's *Portrait of the Artist as a Young Man*:

> I have engaged in silence
> exile and cunning.

whose hero Stephen Dedalus suggests the myth of Daedalus and Icarus:

> I flew too near the sun
> and my wax wings fell off.

and then that hero's reappearance in *Ulysses*:

> I am looking for my Old Man
> whom I never knew.

Walt Whitman's *Leaves of Grass* is here:

> And I may make my notebooks
> into sheaves of grass.

and

> I hear America singing
> in the Yellow Pages.

and "The Sleepers":

> I am the man.
> I was there.
> I suffered
> somewhat.

as well as Allen Ginsberg's "Howl":

> I have heard the Gettysburg Address
> and the Ginsberg Address.

and

> I too have ridden boxcars boxcars boxcars.

These allusions in his poetic "Autobiography" show Ferlinghetti taking on the identities of his cherished writers. Earl Miner, who wrote the book on Japanese court poetry,[11] notes "The technique of allusion assumes: (1) an established literary tradition as a source of value; (2) an audience sharing the tradition with the poet; (3) an echo of sufficiently familiar yet distinctive and meaningful elements; and (4) a fusion of the echo with elements in the new context." Allusive poetry is not experimental or primitive, but classic and complex.

The critic M. L. Rosenthal calls him a "deft, rapid-paced, whirling performer [with] a wonderful eye for meaning in the commonplace."[26] The beloved book *A Coney Island of the Mind* is an essential Beat text, and shows what poetry was in San Francisco in the mid-1950s, when Kerouac, Ginsberg, and Corso arrived from the east and encountered Lawrence Ferlinghetti, painter, poet, translator, publisher: the nexus.

2nd Chorus:
Blues:
Jack Kerouac

There are writers who achieve equally at poetry and prose, like Johann von Goethe and Boris Pasternak, but it's easier to tag a writer as a master at one of these forms and ignore their work in the other, then hide this expedience behind the assumption that no one can achieve at both. And so there are American writers whose verse is eclipsed by their fiction, but not because it's unworthy, and these include Herman Melville, Stephen Crane, and Jack Kerouac. This prejudice accounts for the fact that Kerouac, author of the Beat novel *On the Road,* though he had poetry published, did not see his splendid *Book of Haikus* in print during his life, as it came out forty-two years after it was written. He contended that he didn't distinguish between poetry and prose: in a letter to Ginsberg, he said, "You guys call yourselves poets, write little short lines, I'm a poet but I write lines paragraphs and pages and many pages long."[44]

Consider this passage from *On the Road,* completed in 1952:[27]

27

"We wheeled through the sultry old light of Algiers, back on the ferry, back toward the mud-splashed, crabbed old ships across the river, back on Canal, and out; on a two-lane highway to Baton Rouge in purple darkness; swung west there, crossed the Mississippi at a place called Port Allen. Port Allen—where the river's all rain and roses in a misty pinpoint darkness and where we swung around a circular drive in yellow foglight and suddenly saw the great black body below a bridge and crossed eternity again."

And Regina Weinreich's poetic analysis:[46]

"The repetition of 'back' develops in a typical build-up so that the pacing of the unconscious exposition that follows gains momentum. This momentum is further triggered by the assonance and alliteration that move the line of Kerouac's free prose. The initial *w* and long *e* sounds lead into the slant rhymes of 'ul,' 'ol,' and 'Al.' The short *a* of 'back' is echoed in 'splashed' and 'crabbed,' all intended to emphasize the 'wheeling' motion that he is describing. The use of prepositions—'on,' 'toward,' 'out'—reinforces 'wheeling' so that a great deal of ground is covered in a compact motion.

"Note the pacing in the 'unconscious' exposition that follows. . . First, the repetition of 'Port Allen' creates force. Second, the poetic effects are tighter. The rolling *r*'s of 'where,' 'river,' 'rain,' 'roses,' are picked up by 'darkness,' with 'where' again creating a circular motion. The word 'swung' is repeated; 'around' picks up the rolling *r* as does 'circular drive,' which actually states what the writing accomplishes at the levels of both sound and sense. . . And the alliteration of the *b*'s in 'black body below a bridge' suggests something still mysterious as the passage comes full circle in crossing the Mississippi (and eternity) again."

In theory, Kerouac may consider prose and poetry as the same, but in practice his prose has narrative and characters not found in his poetry, though it can intensify in description through rhetoric and sound into a poetic texture. His poetry, unlike his prose, loosens into free association and free verse. It has the music and compression expected in that genre.

In 1953, Kerouac wrote his first poetic cycle, "Richmond Hill Blues",[31] twenty-two lyric poems with titles, and in the next year he extended that experiment with the eighty choruses of *San Francisco Blues*.[31] Like Ferlinghetti's *Pictures of the gone world*, 1953,[12] it's a numbered series of word paintings of the city, in which individual poems may stand alone or be considered stanzas in a cycle, and whose form is determined spatially. Kerouac says:[31]

> "In my system, the form of blues choruses is limited by the small page of the breastpocket notebook in which they are written, like the form of a set number of bars in a jazz blues chorus, and so sometimes the word-meaning can carry from one chorus into another, or not, just like the phrase-meaning can carry harmonically from one chorus to the other, or not, in jazz, so that, in these blues as in jazz, the form is determined by time, and by the musician's spontaneous phrasing & harmonizing with the beat of the time as it waves & waves on by in measured choruses."

In a May 1954 letter to Ginsberg, Kerouac describes the origin of what he calls his first book of poetry: "This is from my new book of poems *San Francisco Blues* that I wrote when I left Neal's in March and went to live in the Cameo Hotel on Third Street Frisco Skidrow—wrote it in a rockingchair at the window, looking down on winos and bebop winos and whores and Cop cars. . ."[33]

Beat Poetry

70th Chorus

3rd St is like Moody St
Lowell Massachusetts
It has Bagdad blue
  Dusk down sky
  And hills with lights
And pale the hazel
  Gentle blue in the
        burned windows
Of wooden tenements,
  And lights of bars,
        music brawl,
  "Hoap!" "Hap!" & "Hi"
In the street of blood
And bells billygoating
  Boom by at the ache
        of day
The break of personalities
  Crossing just once
  In the wrong door

Each chorus is a quick sketch, looking out the window and, in 70th Chorus, into the sundown sky and rundown street. In 1951, the painter Ed White had suggested to Kerouac, "Just sketch in the streets like a painter but with words,"[47] and a few days later he attempted this new technique. Here's an example from *Visions of Cody*:[28]

> "A sad park of autumn, late Saturday afternoon—leaves by now so dry they make a general rattle all over and a little girl in a green knit cap is squashing leaves against the wire fence and then trying to climb over them—also mothers in the waning light, sitting their kiddies in swing seats of gray iron and pushing them with grave and dutiful playfulness—A little boy in red woodsman shirt stoops to drink water at the dry concrete fountain—a flag whips through the bare bleak branches—salmon is the color of parts of the sky—the children in the swings kick their feet in air, mothers say *Wheee*—a trash wirebasket is half full of dry, dry leaves—a pool of last night's rain lies in the gravel; tonight it will be cold, clear, winter coming and who will haunt the deserted park then?"

70th Chorus is a sketch in verse: offhand, on the spot, spontaneous sight and sound notations, connected paratactically by a dash or "and", but in short, two- to eight-syllable lines, and with the connotative language, compression, and music of poetry. This technique abjures revision, and assumes that a poet can improvise as successfully as a jazz musician: "It's all gotta be non stop ad libbing within each chorus, or the gig is shot."[31] In a letter written when preparing the manuscript for publication, Kerouac notes that he's restored "original lines that I had tried to erase and write over of in 1954!"[33] Improvisation had existed in oral poetry, in primitive song, in Homer's interpolations, where pre-existing material helped shape the poem, and in written Japanese renga, from which the independent haiku emerged, where complex rules were meant to assure form.

Notice that the opening lines of the following chorus,

> Nevermore to remain
> Nevermore to return

can be read as a natural continuation of the last lines of 70th Chorus, where two people cross paths and don't connect. Then there's a dash, and 71st Chorus veers off into an evocation of other rooms in the hotel; however, the riff about Third Street and Moody Street is restated. This raises the question: should 70th Chorus be read alone, or with the first two lines of 71st Chorus, or do both choruses make a poem, or the whole cycle? Kerouac said in a June 1961 letter, "I see it is a beautiful unity,"[33] and in the introduction to *Mexico City Blues*, "I want to be considered a jazz poet blowing a long blues in an afternoon jam session on Sunday."[32] Kerouac blurs the line between prose and poetry, between one poem and the next, and between life and art, because he's not imagining, he's sitting in the rocking chair in the Cameo Hotel, improvising.

The poetry wavers between evocative phrases, "and hills with lights," and light metaphor, "the street of blood." Besides the parallels with Ferlinghetti already outlined, the chorus seems to be influenced by the rich and quick-changing language of Shakespeare in *Hamlet*, 1600:[48]

> And I, of ladies most deject and wretched,
> that suck'd the honey of his music vows,
> now see that noble and most sovereign reason,
> like sweet bells jangled, out of tune and harsh. . .
>
> III. i. 158-161

in phrases like

> music brawl,
> "Hoap!" "Hap!" & "Hi"
> In the street of blood
> And bells billygoating

by translations of Japanese haiku by R. H. Blyth:[49]

Not a single stone
To throw at the dog—
The wintry moon!

Taigi, 18th C.

The silence!
The voice of the cicada
Penetrates the rocks.

Basho, 17th C.

On the sandy beach,
Footprints:
Long is the spring day.

Shiki, 19th C.

in its five triads by indentation:

It has Bagdad blue
Dusk down sky
And hills with lights

and by Ginsberg's 1953 long poem, "The Green Automobile":[53]

But first we'll drive the stations of downtown,
poolhall flophouse jazzjoint jail
whorehouse down Folsom
to the darkest alleys of Larimer

paying respects to Denver's father
lost on the railroad tracks,
stupor of wine and silence
hallowing the slum of his decades,

in its short lines and downbeat city images:

Gentle blue in the
burned windows
Of wooden tenements,

acknowledged by Kerouac: ". . . Allen had influenced me with mad image-makings and crazy 'oops!' writing."[33]

San Francisco Blues was written, according to an April 1962 letter, "with that fuckyou freedom,"[45] which means, "in poetry, you can be completely free to say anything you want, you don't have to tell a story, you can use secret puns. . ."[6] One consequence of freedom from considering the reader is private reference, and the poem begins by comparing the present street with one in memory, whose importance is clear only when it's known that it's his teenage street, and by associating "Bagdad" and "blue," as though from an illustration in a childhood copy of *The Arabian Nights*. The collocation of San Francisco, Lowell, and Bagdad suggest that it doesn't matter what city he's living in, there's always a rundown street, as in Ferlinghetti's "The Long Street":[15]

> The long street
> which is the street of the world

The introduction to the street is one sentence, and the rest of the poem another; light punctuation increases the ambiguity of the phrases. The body of the poem, using alliteration on *b* for all major words, is divided into an evocation of the serenity of nature—"blue dusk," "gentle blue"—and a meditation on the fury of humanity—"brawl," "blood", "billygoating," "boom", "break." The poem is unified by other music, of assonance on *a*, as well, in "pale the hazel," "ache / of day / The break." The alliterative sequence "Hoap!" "Hap!" & "Hi," which are nonsense, is a Kerouac signature, coming from his love of language before semantics; in almost every poem, there is a series of pure sound syllables.

After the peace of the sky at dusk, the poem turns at the "burned windows" in the "wooden tenements," which can be seen as reflecting blue sky and red sunset, or as having been literally burned, or as burning with the fire of neglect. Violence emerges, as out of the bars comes "music brawl," which can be loud music, or music followed by a fight. "'Hoap!' 'Hap!' &

'Hi'", which sound like jazz scat singing, are half-heard words from below, or symbols, monosyllabic and meaningless, of people who fail to communicate, yelled "In the street of blood"; the meanings of the homonyms, hope, hap, and high, are there in undertone.

The bells are the evening angelus, ringing a call to prayer in the down and out Mission district; however, they don't evoke prayer or restore peace: they are "billygoating," an image associated with the devil, or bells on animals, and "boom," like explosions. "The ache of day" is a poignant play on "the break of day"; "break" is then picked up in "The break of personalities," as possible friends or lovers "cross," one going in, one out, in a verb alluding to crucifixion, and fail to connect in their one chance at the entry to the harsh bar, which is "the wrong door."

The name Beat was originally intended by Kerouac to mean beat down; he later revised it to include beatific—in his words, "beat, meaning down and out but full of intense conviction."[34] The "tenements" and "bars" evoke the earlier sense, and "bells" and "crossing" the later. The poet looks out of the skid row hotel window and plays a downhearted solo on the saxophone of our language. That he's not in the street, but at the window, gives a natural aesthetic distance, important to art.

In his Paris Review interview, he equates a stanza with a breath:[6]

"... a tenor man drawing a breath and blowing a phrase on his saxophone, till he runs out of breath, and when he does, his sentence, his statement's been made. . . That's how I therefore separate my sentences, as breath separations of the mind. . . I formulated the theory of breath as measure, in prose and verse, . . . in 1953 at the request of Burroughs and Ginsberg."

If 70th Chorus is rewritten in possible breaths,

It has Bagdad blue dusk down sky and hills with lights
   and pale the hazel gentle blue in the burned

35

windows of wooden tenements,
and lights of bars, music brawl, "Hoap!" "Hap!" & "Hi"
in the street of blood, and bells billygoating
boom by at the ache of day, the break of
personalities crossing just once in the wrong
door

it's the sound of Ginsberg's "Howl":[55]

who walked all night with their shoes full of blood on
the snowbank docks waiting for a door in the
East River to open to a room full of steamheat
and opium,
who created great suicidal dramas on the apartment
cliff-banks of the Hudson under the wartime
blue floodlight of the moon & their heads shall
be crowned with laurel in oblivion

Kerouac was invited by Ginsberg to read at the 6 Gallery event, but said no: ". . . I won't do it because I'm too bashful."[33] He did show up: ". . . the big mad capping final night of the great poetry reading with Allen on the stage before a hundred eager Raskolniks in glasses crowding in from the rear of the reading hall, with wine in my hands a gallon jug I'm drinking yelling 'Go,' Allen is howling his HOWL pome and other crazy poets there, it's mad, it will never end. . ."[33] In October 1957, with Philip Lamantia and Howard Hart, and accompanied by the musician David Amram, Kerouac gave the first New York poetry and jazz reading, at the Brata Art Gallery, of these and other poems. He considered *San Francisco Blues* a major book; with its connections to jazz and oral poetry, it's fitting that though choruses appeared in literary journals, it was rejected by publishers, and appeared, as choruses 1 – 23, on his 1959 recording *Blues and Haikus*,[36] with two saxophones counterpointing and harmonizing; five more choruses appeared in 1960 on *Readings by Jack Kerouac on the Beat Generation*.[37] In 1983 it was bootlegged in Bristol, England, and in 1995 officially published in Kerouac's own anthology of eight blues cycles, *Book of Blues*,[31] which includes "San Francisco Blues", "Richmond Hill Blues", "Bowery Blues", "MacDougal Street Blues", "Desolation Blues", "Orizaba 210 Blues", "Orlanda Blues", "Cerrada Medellin Blues," and not "Berkeley Blues", "Brooklyn Bridge Blues", "Tangier Blues", "Washington DC Blues", "Earthquake Blues". *Mexico City Blues*,[32] the longest cycle, was published in 1960. They are sketches improvised in the places they name, occasionally moving into inward meditations, ordered by the mystery that governs the days in which they were written.

Blues and Haikus has the composite quality seen in many Beat poetry texts, which shows radically different ways of poetry side by side. Kerouac's "blues" are redefined by him, and only have improvisation and low-down feeling in common with the musical form. In the same way, his "haikus" are redefined by him, and may only have the stanza, three short lines, in common with the Japanese poetic form:[43]

"The 'haiku' was invented and developed over hundreds of years in Japan to be a complete poem in seventeen syllables and to pack in a whole vision of life in three short lines. A 'Western Haiku' need not concern itself with the seventeen syllables since Western languages cannot adapt themselves to the fluid syllabic Japanese. I propose that the 'Western Haiku' simply say a lot in three short lines in any Western language.

"Above all, a Haiku must be very simple and free of all poetic trickery and make a little picture and yet be as airy and graceful as a Vivaldi Pastorella. Here is a great Japanese Haiku that is simpler and prettier than any Haiku I could ever write in any language:—

A day of quiet gladness,—
Mount Fuji is veiled
In misty rain.

(Basho) (1644-1694)

Here is another. . .

She has put the child to sleep,
And now washes the clothes;
The summer moon.

(Issa) (1763-1827)

And another, by Buson (1715-1783):

The nightingale is singing,
Its small mouth,
Open."

He's outlining his inspirations, discovered in volumes of haiku translated by R. H. Blyth[50]. He read these books with his friends, Gary Snyder, Allen Ginsberg, and Philip Whalen, in Berkeley, 1955. Kerouac, from the east, found himself as a poet in the west, and improvised street poetry, called blues, but he also worked in the tight form of Western "haikus", as he acknowledges in his essay "The Origins of Joy in Poetry":[43]

"The new American poetry as typified by the SF Renaissance (which means Ginsberg, me, Rexroth, Ferlinghetti, McClure, Corso, Gary Snyder, Philip Lamantia, Philip Whalen, I guess) is a kind of new-old Zen Lunacy poetry, writing whatever comes into your head as it comes, poetry returned to its origin, in the bardic child, truly ORAL as Ferling said, instead of gray faced Academic quibbling. . . But SF is the poetry of a new Holy Lunacy like that of ancient times (Li Po, Han Shan, Tom o Bedlam, Kit Smart, Blake) yet it also has that mental discipline typified by the haiku (Basho, Buson), that is, the discipline of pointing out things directly, purely, concretely, no abstractions or explanations, wham

wham the true blue song of man."

Here are ten consecutive poems from *Book of Haikus*:[38]

Missing a kick
   at the icebox door
It closed anyway

Perfect moonlit night
   marred
By family squabbles

The Spring moon—
   How many miles away
Those orange blossoms!

When the moon sinks
   down to the power line,
I'll go in

Looking up at the stars,
   feeling sad,
Going "tsk tsk tsk"

This July evening,
   A large frog
On my doorsill!

Dawn, a falling star
   —A dewdrop lands
On my head!

In back of the Supermarket,
   in the parking lot weeds,
Purple flowers

Protected by the clouds,
   the moon
Sleeps sailing

Chief Crazy Horse
   looks tearfully north
The first snow flurries

Earl Miner, author of *Japanese Court Poetry*, notes that haiku in the West keep the concreteness and compression of their Japanese models, but that they're an attempt to graft the exotic Eastern form onto the Western lyric, which doesn't take, and the results are trivial: "Haiku is too reduced a form and grows too complexly out of its cultural background to be adaptable as a whole into Western languages."[11] He's referring to haiku's roots in the larger forms of renga and tanka, its syllabic music, and its allusiveness. But Kerouac transforms all he touches. Given modern prose, he improvises sketches; given the blues, he writes notebook page poetry; and so, given haiku, rather than repeating the failure Miner points out, he tries to reinvent it as a Western form. It isn't about seasonal words or seventeen syllables, but it keeps the Zen objectivity praised in Basho by his favored translator, R. H. Blyth,[49] whether Basho is looking at the object

> "By the roadside,
>   A Rose of Sharon;
>   The horse has eaten it.
>   . . . (There is colour, there is movement; the horse's strange, rubber-like nose nuzzling the flower; no poet anywhere to be seen.)"

or the subject

> "Leaves of the willow tree fall;
>   The master and I stand listening
>   To the sound of the bell.
>   . . . (The ear full of sound; the heart full of silence; the communion of saints.)"

Kerouac, in a notebook, describes this method: "Keep the eye STEADILY on the object."[38] This leads to concreteness, where the senses are always engaged; when he says "pack in," this leads to compression, where the music is in the scarcity of syllables. In so few words, distributed alliteration, as in "moonlit night / marred," and assonance, as in "Horse / looks tearfully north", are intensified. In "Perfect moonlit night / marred / By family squabbles," we imagine outdoors and indoors, see the moon's grace and hear the husband and wife, or father and son, yelling; we feel the distance between the moon on its way, and the family in disharmony. Kerouac's haikus span the worlds of nature: moon, blossoms, stars, frog, dewdrop, weeds, flowers, clouds, snow; and man: icebox, family, power line, doorsill, supermarket, Crazy Horse.

"Missing a kick / at the icebox door / It closed anyway" appears to lack imagery from nature, until it's seen that the physics of the spring that closes the door is natural, and that the point is that, as the Tao Te Ching says, inaction when appropriate is fine, since "Good government comes of itself."[51] The haiku "Chief Crazy Horse / looks tearfully north / The first snow flurries" which Kerouac thought his best, is an historical epic in three lines that hold the uncertain stand, the nobility, and the final grief, of the American Indians.

Kerouac speaks of discipline in relation to haiku, and invokes concreteness and compression. It's a revelation to find that this writer, associated with spontaneous prose and poetry, recommends revision when writing in this form: ". . . haiku is best reworked and revised."[6] In this interview, he goes on to compose a haiku, recasting and paring the lines. This artifice can be seen inside one haiku, or the whole series. There is a sequence in the haikus quoted: kitchen, home in moonlight, moon, stars, evening, morning, flowers, the moon and sleep, a dream of history. *Book of Haikus* is composed. He follows, not the laws, but the spirit, of the haiku, knowing that a masterpiece makes its own laws.

The modernists were influenced by haiku, with a few memorable results: Ezra Pound's "In a Station of the Metro," 1912, Wallace Stevens' "Thirteen Ways of Looking at a Blackbird," 1917, William Carlos Williams' "The Red Wheelbarrow," 1923. Earl Miner asserts that Pound's idea of "super-position," where the objective transforms into the subjective, was modeled on haiku, and informs his later work.[11] But Kerouac devoted himself to haiku, and wrote and rewrote hundreds of them, arranging them into books.

The "haikus" written from 1956 to 1961, in the shirt pocket notebooks with sketches and blues, were selected, revised, and sequenced for *Book of Haikus*, which was rejected by publishers, and published, in part, on the same 1959 recording as *San Francisco Blues, Blues and Haikus*.[36] His performance there, with saxophone players alternating at improvising responses, is extraordinary. Talking about the Beat poets reading out loud to jazz, David Meltzer says, Kerouac "had the truest ear and spirit for it, his language responding to the music easily. His work on record with Al Cohn and Zoot Sims displayed some lovely possibilities."[21] Because I could no longer wait for the publication of Kerouac's lost book, I selected and calligraphed *American Haikus*, in 1992. The complete *Book of Haikus*,[38] with 213 poems on a world of subjects, was published in 2003 as one of the sections of *Book of Haikus*, with two later manuscripts, *Desolation Pops* and *Beat Generation Haikus*, and uncollected haikus gathered from his notebooks and prose.

Regina Weinreich summarizes Kerouac's achievement, in form: "the purposeful caesura or cut of Japanese haiku as key to its sound and sense"; and in content: "the rendering of a subject's essence, and the shimmering, ephemeral nature of its fleeting existence."[38] Both can be seen in the haiku

> In back of the Supermarket,
>   in the parking lot weeds,
> Purple flowers

where the cut comes between "weeds" and "Purple flowers"; the nature of flowers, "born to blush unseen," is encountered in the neglected lot. Kerouac's haikus are like those flowers: everyone's in the supermarket, and they bloom anyway. Ginsberg says of Kerouac, "In addition he has the one sure sign of being a great poet, which is he's the only one in the United States who knows how to write haiku."[6] There is nothing like *Book of Haikus* in our literature: it's an American classic. What did Kerouac say? "Come back and tell me in a hundred years."[44]

3rd Chorus:
Howl:
Allen Ginsberg

In the liner notes to the recordings *Howl and Other Poems*[2] and *Holy Soul Jelly Roll*,[59] and "Author's Preface: Reader's Guide" to *Howl: Original Draft Facsimile*,[54] Allen Ginsberg tells of the poem's origin:

> "By 1955 I wrote poetry adapted from prose seeds, journals, scratchings, arranged by phrasing or breath groups into little short-line patterns according to ideas of measure of American speech I'd picked up from W. C. Williams' imagist preoccupations. I suddenly turned aside in San Francisco, unemployment compensation leisure, to follow my romantic inspiration—Hebraic-Melvillian bardic breath. . . I had recently dreamt of the late Joan Burroughs, a sympathetic encounter with her spirit. . . She asked me what'd happened to Bill, Herbert Huncke, Lucien Carr, and Kerouac. Dreaming, I realized she was dead and asked, 'What do you remember of the living?'

and saw a sudden 'jump cut' vision of an old crooked-branched tree rising above her tombstone. That gave me the idea of a quick shift from one visual image to another. . . I wrote the dream as a poem ('Dream Record: June 8, 1955'), about which in a few days Kenneth Rexroth, an elder in this literary city, wrote me he thought was stilted & somewhat academic. A week later, I sat idly at my desk by the first-floor window facing Montgomery Street's slope to gay Broadway—only a few blocks from City Lights literary paperback bookshop. I had a secondhand typewriter, some cheap scratch paper. . . I thought I wouldn't write a <u>poem</u>, but just write what I wanted to without fear, let my imagination go, open secrecy, and scribble magic lines from my real mind—sum up my life—something I wouldn't be able to show anybody, writ for my own soul's ear and a few other golden ears. So the first line of Howl, 'I saw the best minds etc.', the whole first section typed out madly in one afternoon, a huge sad comedy of wild phrasing, meaningless images for the beauty of abstract poetry of mind running along making awkward combinations like Charlie Chaplin's walk, long saxophone-like chorus lines I knew Kerouac would hear *sound* of—taking off from his own inspired prose line really a new poetry."

Ginsberg had tacked up in his room Jack Kerouac's "Belief & Technique for Modern Prose*****List of Essentials",[33] which included these lines:

"1. <u>Scribbled</u> <u>secret</u> notebooks, and wild typewritten pages, for yr <u>own</u> joy

4. Be in love with yr <u>life</u>

8. <u>Write</u> <u>what</u> <u>you</u> <u>want</u> bottomless from bottom of the <u>mind</u>

24. No <u>fear</u> or shame in the dignity of yr experience, language & knowledge"

Ginsberg echoes Kerouac in his account of the seeding of "Howl": "I thought I wouldn't write a *poem*, but just <u>write</u> <u>what</u> <u>I</u> <u>wanted</u> to without <u>fear</u>, let my imagination go, open <u>secrecy</u>, and <u>scribble</u> magic lines from my real <u>mind</u>—sum up my <u>life</u>— something I wouldn't be able to show anybody, writ for my <u>own</u> soul's ear. . ." In a letter to him he acknowledges, ". . . how right you are, that was the first time I sat down to blow, it came out in your method, sounding like you, an imitation practically."[33] He took Kerouac's directives to heart, and wrote "Howl" Part I, then mailed this first draft to Kerouac in Mexico City:

> I saw the best minds of my generation
> generation destroyed by madness
> starving, mystical, naked,
> who dragged themselves thru the angry streets at
> dawn looking for a negro fix
> who poverty and tatters and fantastic minds
> sat up all night in lofts
> contemplating jazz,
> who bared their brains to heaven under the El
> and saw Mohammedan angels staggering
> on tenement roofs illuminated,

This poem was revised over the next year, till it was published:[55]

HOWL

For
Carl Solomon

I

I saw the best minds of my generation destroyed by madness,
starving hysterical naked,
dragging themselves through the negro streets at dawn looking
for an angry fix,
angelheaded hipsters burning for the ancient heavenly connection
to the starry dynamo in the machinery of night,
who poverty and tatters and hollow-eyed and high sat up smoking
in the supernatural darkness of cold-water flats floating
across the tops of cities contemplating jazz,
who bared their brains to Heaven under the El and saw
Mohammedan angels staggering on tenement roofs
illuminated,
who passed through universities with radiant cool eyes
hallucinating Arkansas and Blake-light tragedy among
the scholars of war,
who were expelled from the academies for crazy & publishing
obscene odes on the windows of the skull,
who cowered in unshaven rooms in underwear, burning their
money in wastebaskets and listening to the Terror through
the wall,
who got busted in their pubic beards returning through Laredo
with a belt of marijuana for New York,
who ate fire in paint hotels or drank turpentine in Paradise Alley,
death, or purgatoried their torsos night after night
with dreams, with drugs, with waking nightmares, alcohol and
cock and endless balls,
incomparable blind streets of shuddering cloud and lightning in
the mind leaping toward poles of Canada & Paterson,
illuminating all the motionless world of Time between,
Peyote solidities of halls, backyard green tree cemetery dawns,

46

wine drunkenness over the rooftops, storefront boroughs
of teahead joyride neon blinking traffic light, sun and
moon and tree vibrations in the roaring winter dusks of
Brooklyn, ashcan rantings and kind king light of mind,

who chained themselves to subways for the endless ride from
Battery to holy Bronx on benzedrine until the noise of
wheels and children brought them down shuddering
mouth-wracked and battered bleak of brain all drained
of brilliance in the drear light of Zoo,

who sank all night in submarine light of Bickford's floated out and
sat through the stale beer afternoon in desolate Fugazzi's,
listening to the crack of doom on the hydrogen jukebox,

who talked continuously seventy hours from park to pad to bar
to Bellevue to museum to the Brooklyn Bridge,

a lost battalion of platonic conversationalists jumping down the
stoops off fire escapes off windowsills off Empire State
out of the moon,

yacketayakking screaming vomiting whispering facts and
memories and anecdotes and eyeball kicks and shocks of
hospitals and jails and wars,

whole intellects disgorged in total recall for seven days and
nights with brilliant eyes, meat for the Synagogue cast
on the pavement,

who vanished into nowhere Zen New Jersey leaving a trail of
ambiguous picture postcards of Atlantic City Hall,

suffering Eastern sweats and Tangerian bone-grindings and
migraines of China under junk-withdrawal in Newark's
bleak furnished room,

who wandered around and around at midnight in the railroad
yard wondering where to go, and went, leaving no broken
hearts,

who lit cigarettes in boxcars boxcars boxcars racketing through
snow toward lonesome farms in grandfather night,

who studied Plotinus Poe St. John of the Cross telepathy and
bop kabbalah because the cosmos instinctively vibrated
at their feet in Kansas,

who loned it through the streets of Idaho seeking visionary indian

47

angels who were visionary indian angels,

who thought they were only mad when Baltimore gleamed in supernatural ecstasy,

who jumped in limousines with the Chinaman of Oklahoma on the impulse of winter midnight streetlight smalltown rain,

who lounged hungry and lonesome through Houston seeking jazz or sex or soup, and followed the brilliant Spaniard to converse about America and Eternity, a hopeless task, and so took ship to Africa,

who disappeared into the volcanoes of Mexico leaving behind nothing but the shadow of dungarees and the lava and ash of poetry scattered in fireplace Chicago,

who reappeared on the West Coast investigating the F.B.I. in beards and shorts with big pacifist eyes sexy in their dark skin passing out incomprehensible leaflets,

who burned cigarette holes in their arms protesting the narcotic tobacco haze of Capitalism,

who distributed Supercommunist pamphlets in Union Square weeping and undressing while the sirens of Los Alamos wailed them down, and wailed down Wall, and the Staten Island ferry also wailed,

who broke down crying in white gymnasiums naked and trembling before the machinery of other skeletons,

who bit detectives in the neck and shrieked with delight in policecars for committing no crime but their own wild cooking pederasty and intoxication,

who howled on their knees in the subway and were dragged off the roof waving genitals and manuscripts,

who let themselves be fucked in the ass by saintly motorcyclists, and screamed with joy,

who blew and were blown by those human seraphim, the sailors, caresses of Atlantic and Caribbean love,

who balled in the morning in the evenings in rosegardens and the grass of public parks and cemeteries scattering their semen freely to whomever come who may,

who hiccuped endlessly trying to giggle but wound up with a

sob behind a partition in a Turkish Bath when the blond
& naked angel came to pierce them with a sword,

who lost their loveboys to the three old shrews of fate the one
eyed shrew of the heterosexual dollar the one eyed shrew
that winks out of the womb and the one eyed shrew that
does nothing but sit on her ass and snip the intellectual
golden threads of the craftsman's loom,

who copulated ecstatic and insatiate with a bottle of beer a
sweetheart a package of cigarettes a candle and fell off
the bed, and continued along the floor and down the hall
and ended fainting on the wall with a vision of ultimate
cunt and come eluding the last gyzym of consciousness,

who sweetened the snatches of a million girls trembling in the
sunset, and were red eyed in the morning but prepared
to sweeten the snatch of the sunrise, flashing buttocks
under barns and naked in the lake,

who went out whoring through Colorado in myriad stolen night-
cars, N.C., secret hero of these poems, cocksman and
Adonis of Denver—joy to the memory of his innumerable
lays of girls in empty lots & diner backyards, moviehouses'
rickety rows, on mountaintops in caves or with gaunt
waitresses in familiar roadside lonely petticoat upliftings
& especially secret gas-station solipsisms of johns, &
hometown alleys too,

who faded out in vast sordid movies, were shifted in dreams,
woke on a sudden Manhattan, and picked themselves
up out of basements hung over with heartless Tokay
and horrors of Third Avenue iron dreams & stumbled to
unemployment offices,

who walked all night with their shoes full of blood on the
snowbank docks waiting for a door in the East River to
open to a room full of steamheat and opium,

who created great suicidal dramas on the apartment cliff-banks
of the Hudson under the wartime blue floodlight of the
moon & their heads shall be crowned with laurel in
oblivion,

who ate the lamb stew of the imagination or digested the crab at the muddy bottom of the rivers of Bowery,

who wept at the romance of the streets with their pushcarts full of onions and bad music,

who sat in boxes breathing in the darkness under the bridge, and rose up to build harpsichords in their lofts,

who coughed on the sixth floor of Harlem crowned with flame under the tubercular sky surrounded by orange crates of theology,

who scribbled all night rocking and rolling over lofty incantations which in the yellow morning were stanzas of gibberish,

who cooked rotten animals lung heart feet tail borsht & tortillas dreaming of the pure vegetable kingdom,

who plunged themselves under meat trucks looking for an egg,

who threw their watches off the roof to cast their ballot for Eternity outside of Time, & alarm clocks fell on their heads every day for the next decade,

who cut their wrists three times successively unsuccessfully, gave up and were forced to open antique stores where they thought they were growing old and cried,

who were burned alive in their innocent flannel suits on Madison Avenue amid blasts of leaden verse & the tanked-up clatter of the iron regiments of fashion & the nitroglycerine shrieks of the fairies of advertising & the mustard gas of sinister intelligent editors, or were run down by the drunken taxicabs of Absolute Reality,

who jumped off the Brooklyn Bridge this actually happened and walked away unknown and forgotten into the ghostly daze of Chinatown soup alleyways & firetrucks, not even one free beer,

who sang out of their windows in despair, fell out of the subway window, jumped in the filthy Passaic, leaped on negroes, cried all over the street, danced on broken wineglasses barefoot smashed phonograph records of nostalgic European 1930s German jazz finished the whiskey and threw up groaning into the bloody toilet, moans in their ears and the blast of colossal steam whistles,

who barreled down the highways of the past journeying to

each other's hotrod-Golgotha jail-solitude watch or Birmingham jazz incarnation,

who drove crosscountry seventytwo hours to find out if I had a vision or you had a vision or he had a vision to find out Eternity,

who journeyed to Denver, who died in Denver, who came back to Denver & waited in vain, who watched over Denver & brooded & loned in Denver and finally went away to find out the Time, & now Denver is lonesome for her heroes,

who fell on their knees in hopeless cathedrals praying for each other's salvation and light and breasts, until the soul illuminated its hair for a second,

who crashed through their minds in jail waiting for impossible criminals with golden heads and the charm of reality in their hearts who sang sweet blues to Alcatraz,

who retired to Mexico to cultivate a habit, or Rocky Mount to tender Buddha or Tangiers to boys or Southern Pacific to the black locomotive or Harvard to Narcissus to Woodlawn to the daisychain or grave,

who demanded sanity trials accusing the radio of hypnotism & were left with their insanity & their hands & a hung jury,

who threw potato salad at CCNY lecturers on Dadaism and subsequently presented themselves on the granite steps of the madhouse with shaven heads and harlequin speech of suicide, demanding instantaneous lobotomy,

and who were given instead the concrete void of insulin Metrazol electricity hydrotherapy psychotherapy occupational therapy pingpong & amnesia,

who in humorless protest overturned only one symbolic pingpong table, resting briefly in catatonia,

returning years later truly bald except for a wig of blood, and tears and fingers, to the visible madman doom of the wards of the madtowns of the East,

Pilgrim State's Rockland's and Greystone's foetid halls, bickering with the echoes of the soul, rocking and rolling in the

midnight solitude-bench dolmen-realms of love, dream
of life a nightmare, bodies turned to stone as heavy as
the moon,

with mother finally ******, and the last fantastic book flung out
of the tenement window, and the last door closed at 4.
A.M. and the last telephone slammed at the wall in reply
and the last furnished room emptied down to the last
piece of mental furniture, a yellow paper rose twisted
on a wire hanger in the closet, and even that imaginary,
nothing but a hopeful little bit of hallucination—

ah, Carl, while you are not safe I am not safe, and now you're
really in the total animal soup of time—

and who therefore ran through the icy streets obsessed with a
sudden flash of the alchemy of the use of the ellipse the
catalog the meter & the vibrating plane,

who dreamt and made incarnate gaps in Time & Space through
images juxtaposed, and trapped the archangel of the soul
between 2 visual images and joined the elemental verbs
and set the noun and dash of consciousness together
jumping with sensation of Pater Omnipotens Aeterna
Deus

to recreate the syntax and measure of poor human prose and stand
before you speechless and intelligent and shaking with
shame, rejected yet confessing out the soul to conform to
the rhythm of thought in his naked and endless head,

the madman bum and angel beat in Time, unknown, yet putting
down here what might be left to say in time come after
death,

and rose reincarnate in the ghostly clothes of jazz in the goldhorn
shadow of the band and blew the suffering of America's
naked mind for love into an eli eli lamma lamma
sabacthani saxophone cry that shivered the cities down
to the last radio

with the absolute heart of the poem of life butchered out of their
own bodies good to eat a thousand years.

San Francisco 1955-56

This is unique in English-language poetry for freedom and ambition: one sentence, twelve pages long in its original edition; seventy-eight prose poetry verses, blowing past the traditional short line; its subject and predicate, "I saw"; its anaphora, "who," always bringing the poem back to the human; its range, America and its continent. Its content is as free and ambitious as the country; not fictive, but naked: "confessing out the soul to conform to the rhythm of thought in his naked and endless head." Its diction, unlike the tradition, is naked: cock, fucked, cunt, come. Its bravery and scale say major. It achieves its aim of long jazz saxophone choruses varying a theme. It's too large to annotate or meditate in this context; it needs its own book. Like Stravinsky's *The Rite of Spring*, this work is continuously inspired.

"The poem of life" talks about actual people: William Burroughs, Neal Cassady, Naomi Ginsberg, Carl Solomon. Contingencies are transcended in classic poetry. Here, though confessed as actual, these people are not given as fact, but are unnamed, "N.C.," projected, "secret hero," and mythologized, "Adonis of Denver." The poem sways between metonymy, as when "who dragged themselves thru the angry streets at / dawn looking for a negro fix" is revised to "dragging themselves through the negro streets at dawn looking for an angry fix," and surrealist metaphor, as in "listening to the crack of doom on the hydrogen jukebox." In both figures, the language is opened up in significance: the streets are angry and black, belonging to the dispossessed negroes; the drug injection release is out of rage and darkness; the hydrogen bomb's violence crackles in the blast of rock-and-roll from the jukebox.

In *Howl: Original Draft Facsimile*,[54] Ginsberg lists "Model Texts: Inspirations Precursor to Howl," including poems by Whitman ("a mountain too vast to be seen"), Smart, Shelley, Apollinaire, Schwitters, Mayakovsky, Artaud, Lorca, Crane, Williams. Out of anxiety of influence, he never names the poem's direct model, Kenneth Rexroth's "Thou Shalt Not Kill".[3] Written two years before by the older San Francisco poet, and itself derived from the 16th century poem "Lament of the Makeris" by William Dunbar, whose refrain it quotes, this poet complains that the best minds of his generation are being destroyed:

> They are murdering all the young men.

He uses anaphora, the device of repetition at the beginning of lines:

> How many stopped writing at thirty?
> How many went to work for Time?

He invokes communism, lobotomy, and madness:

> How many died of prefrontal
> Lobotomies in the Communist Party?
> How many are lost in the back roads
> Of provincial madhouses?

He refers to the child sacrifice god of the Old Testament used by Ginsberg in "Howl" Part II:

> stuffed down the maw of Moloch.

The form of "Howl," and its naked content, is derived from the catalog poetry of Walt Whitman, as in "From Pent-Up Aching Rivers," in *Leaves of Grass, Book IV: Children of Adam* (1860):[60]

> From sex, from the warp and from the woof,
> From privacy, from frequent repinings alone,
> From plenty of persons near and yet the right person
> not near,
> From the soft sliding of hands over me and thrusting of
> fingers through my hair and beard,

with Whitman's repetitions stemming from the chant of the King James Old Testament, as in Psalm 103:[61]

> Who forgiveth all thine iniquities; who healeth all thy
> diseases;
> Who redeemeth thy life from destruction; who
> crowneth thee with loving kindness and tender
> mercies;
> Who satisfieth thy mouth with good things; so that thy
> youth is renewed like the eagle's.

Ginsberg adopts the repetition, and the nakedness, of Whitman and David:

> who broke down crying in white gymnasiums naked
> and trembling before the machinery of other
> skeletons,
> who bit detectives in the neck and shrieked with delight
> in policecars for committing no crime but their
> own wild cooking pederasty and intoxication,

He unconsciously echoes his poem's clear predecessor, Hart Crane's *The Bridge* (1930),[62]

> Down Wall, from girder into street noon leaks,

in

> the sirens of Los Alamos wailed them down, and wailed
> down Wall,

The sound in the first draft is derived from W. C. Williams, and his undefinable "variable foot" and "triadic stanza," best heard in his late masterpiece, "Asphodel, That Greeny Flower," written two years before, and published in *Journey to Love* (1955):[63]

> Of asphodel, that greeny flower,
> like a buttercup
> upon its branching stem—

55

> save that it's green and wooden—
>   I come, my sweet,
>   to sing to you.

Ginsberg begins with the stanza, and the honesty, of Williams:

> & the last door closed at four AM and the last
>   companion flown West and the last
>   telephone slammed at the wall
>   in reply and the last furnished room
>   bared to the last piece of
> a mental furniture
>   a yellow paper rose twisted on
>   a wire hanger, in the closet,

When he refers to N. C. as the secret hero of "these poems," he's referring to the beat hero Neal Cassady as an inspiration for Jack Kerouac's *On the Road* (1952), considered as poetry, as well as "Howl." In a letter already quoted, Kerouac wrote, "I'm a poet but I write lines paragraphs. . ." Ginsberg's next composition was the new long lines of "Howl." In the finished poem, Ginsberg fuses the Williams stanza into verse paragraphs which run on, echoing the rhapsody of Kerouac, as in *On the Road*, Chapter 1:[27]

> "But then they danced down the streets like dingledodies and I shambled after as I've been doing all my life after people who interest me, because the only people for me are the mad ones, the ones who are mad to live, mad to talk, mad to be saved, desirous of everything at the same time, the ones who never yawn or say a commonplace thing but burn, burn, burn like fabulous yellow roman candles exploding like spiders across the stars and in the middle you see the blue centerlight and everybody goes 'Aww!'"

Here Ginsberg adopts the long breath, and the improvisation, of

Kerouac:

> angelheaded hipsters burning for the ancient heavenly
>   connection to the starry dynamo in the
>   machinery of night,
> who poverty and tatters and hollow-eyed and high sat
>   up smoking in the supernatural darkness of
>   cold-water flats floating across the tops of cities
>   contemplating jazz,
> who bared their brains to Heaven under the El and saw
>   Mohammedan angels staggering on tenement
>   roofs illuminated,

This apparently prose rhythm in fact doesn't stray far from
Elizabethan blank verse:

> I saw the best minds of my generation
> destroyed by madness, starving hysterical
> naked, dragging themselves through the negro
> streets at dawn looking for an angry fix,
> angelheaded hipsters burning for
> the ancient heavenly connection to
> the starry dynamo in the machinery
> of night, who poverty and tatters and
> hollow-eyed and high sat
> up smoking in the supernatural darkness
> of cold-water flats floating across
> the tops of cities contemplating jazz,
> who bared their brains to Heaven under the El
> and saw Mohammedan angels staggering
> on tenement roofs illuminated, who passed
> through universities with radiant cool eyes

The patterns of music are here as well; in scattered assonance:
"best / generation / hysterical / themselves / angelheaded /
heavenly"; and internal alliteration: "best / destroyed / starving /
streets / hipsters / starry."

Under this is the structure and prophetic tone of the Old Testament, as in Isaiah 13: 19 – 22:[61]

> And Babylon, the glory of kingdoms, the beauty of the
>> Chaldees' excellency, shall be as when God
>> overthrew Sodom and Gomorrah.
> It shall never be inhabited, neither shall it be dwelt in
>> from generation to generation: neither shall the
>> Arabian pitch tent there; neither shall the
>> shepherds make their fold there.
> But wild beasts of the desert shall lie there; and their
>> houses shall be full of doleful creatures; and
>> owls shall dwell there, and satyrs shall dance
>> there.
> And the wild beasts of the islands shall cry in their
>> desolate houses, and dragons in their pleasant
>> palaces: and her time is near to come, and her
>> days shall not be prolonged.

Old Testament prophecy has the diction of extremity: in intensity, because of the urgency of what is said of what is or is to come, and in generality, with plural and collective nouns pointing to what is true for many. For intensity: "glory, beauty, excellency, overthrew, never, wild, full, doleful, desolate"; for generality: "kingdoms, Chaldees, never, generation, Arabian, shepherds, beasts, houses, creatures, owls, satyrs, islands, dragons, palaces, days."

Ginsberg is crying out against a modern Babylon:

> I saw the best minds of my generation destroyed by
>> madness, starving hysterical naked,
> dragging themselves through the negro streets at dawn
>> looking for an angry fix,
> angelheaded hipsters burning for the ancient heavenly
>> connection to the starry dynamo in the
>> machinery of night,
> who poverty and tatters and hollow-eyed and high sat

up smoking in the supernatural darkness of
cold-water flats floating across the tops of cities
contemplating jazz,
who bared their brains to Heaven under the El and saw
Mohammedan angels staggering on tenement
roofs illuminated,

For intensity: "best, destroyed, madness, starving, hysterical, naked, angry, angelheaded, burning, ancient, heavenly, dynamo, poverty, tatters, hollow-eyed, high, supernatural, tops, bared, Heaven"; for generality: "minds, generation, streets, hipsters, flats, tops, cities, brains, angels, roofs." This was recognized immediately by Kerouac, saying the poem ". . .has that right sound of genuine eloquent raging appeal, like Jewish Prophets of Old."[33]

"Howl" has a three-fold structure: I) indictment of a world gone wrong; II) naming of the guilty; III) reaching out to the victims. It's written "for Carl Solomon," who in Part III is seen as a mental patient confined in Rockland Hospital, but the poem immediately extends itself to the madness of "the best minds of my generation," and then portrays examples, as in lines one to eighteen. At first, this madness is understood as clinical insanity, borne out in the language: "hollow-eyed, saw Mohammedan angels, crazy, battered bleak of brain, jumping. . . off Empire State"; these people are reduced to infantile helplessness: "starving hysterical naked"; and release is looked for in the artificial paradise of drugs, in the "angry fix." But "madness" comes to mean not only disease, but a mystical opposition to the dominant materialist culture: "angelheaded, heavenly connection, supernatural darkness, contemplating jazz, Heaven, Mohammedan angels, illuminated". Both disease and mysticism are an indictment of the way of the world, the one a passive downfall, the other an active rebellion.

Now "starving" is reread as dropping out of capitalism, like a starving artist; "hysterical" as passionate; "naked" as honest. All this is derived from Kerouac's double definition of beat: "down and out but full of intense conviction."[24] "Starving" goes on in the thread "looking for, burning for, poverty and tatters, cold-water flats, tenement roofs, unshaven rooms, paint hotels, ashcan, desolate"; "hysterical" in "angry, burning, radiant, hallucinating, crazy, cowered, Terror, ate fire, drank turpentine, purgatoried, nightmares, shuddering, drunkenness, battered, crack of doom, screaming"; and "naked" in "bared, obscene, underwear, pubic, torsos, cock, balls, vomiting whispering facts". These rebels are disengaged from the vapid mainstream culture of purchasing, instead "starving" and "burning their money"; of bland entertainment, instead "hysterical" with "endless balls"; and of hypocrisy, instead "naked" with "memories and anecdotes and eyeball kicks and shocks": they look for an "angry fix, the ancient heavenly connection, contemplating jazz, angels, Blake-light tragedy, lightning in the mind".

The poem in passing sets up the opposition of the academy and the street, as with Ferlinghetti's "long street"[15] and Kerouac's "3rd St",[31] and siding with the street: the "best minds" "passed through universities" and were "expelled from the academies" to go "dragging themselves through the negro streets," "Paradise Alley," "incomparable blind streets," because of the moral failure of the "scholars of war" who consider their odes "obscene." Their new consciousness is reached for through drugs: "fix, hipsters, connection, high, smoking, hallucinating, marijuana, fire, turpentine, drugs, alcohol, Peyote, wine, teahead, benzedrine, beer." They don't live in suburban homes, but in "cold-water flats, unshaven rooms, pads"; they don't drive to work in the morning, but drag themselves through the streets looking for a fix; they take Benzedrine and joyride the subways all day, ranting, in ordinary "halls, backyards, rooftops, storefronts, stoops, fire escapes, windowsills"; at night, they hang out in cafeterias and clubs, get high, listen to jazz, rejecting the world that tries to cage them in "hospitals and jails and wars."

The form of "Howl" began as the episodic Part I, moving between madness as affliction and liberty in the unconventional lives of his contemporaries, evoked in poetry in the same key, to sexual joy, embodied in the "secret hero of these poems." Ginsberg made several attempts to extend this poem, including

"Footnote to Howl," "Fragment 1956," "Many Loves,"and "The Names,"[57] while writing Part II, pointing out the spirit of negation in society, rolled up into the biblical Moloch, and Part III, evoking the lived madness of his mother and his friend in Pilgrim State Hospital, in a psalm of compassion. In the last lines, the madman, free of the madhouse, unites the American East with the West, like Lowell's Kerouac, New York's Corso, Newark's Ginsberg, writing in San Francisco, by an *On the Road* journey:

> in my dreams you walk dripping from a sea-journey on the highway across America in tears to the door of my cottage in the Western night

Allen Ginsberg published "Howl" Part I in 1955 by reciting it at the principal event in Beat literature, the 6 Poets at 6 Gallery reading, introduced by Kenneth Rexroth, with Philip Lamantia, Michael McClure, Philip Whalen, Gary Snyder, Jack Kerouac beating on a wine jug, scat-singing and yelling "Go!" and "Yeah!" before each verse, and Lawrence Ferlinghetti in the audience. It's best related in McClure's memoir, *Scratching the Beat Surface*,[64] and Jack Kerouac's novel, *The Dharma Bums*.[30] That night, Ferlinghetti, quoting Emerson's letter in response to Whitman's *Leaves of Grass*, telegraphed Ginsberg: "I greet you at the beginning of a great career. When do I get the manuscript?"[23] The following year, the first complete reading, in Berkeley, was recorded;[59] three years later, Ginsberg gave the full-breathed performance which was issued on an album named after the book.[58]

For *Howl and Other Poems*, his publisher Ferlinghetti talked Ginsberg out of including the fine earlier long poem "The Green Automobile," and into "In the Baggage Room at the Greyhound" and the downbeat satire "America." People watch tv, but in this poem he warps the expression to mirror his alienation from media and establishment:

America this is the impression I get from looking in the
television set.

The book is in two contrasting sections, like many in Beat
poetry: the first, experimental long-line poems, and the second,
early lyrical pastiches of William Carlos Williams, the last of
which, "In back of the real," is a short-line version of the funky,
rhapsodic poem that most rivals "Howl," "Sunflower Sutra," in
which Kerouac appears. It begins:

> I walked on the banks of the tincan banana dock and
>   sat down under the huge shade of a Southern
>   Pacific locomotive to look at the sunset over the
>   box house hills and cry.
> Jack Kerouac sat beside me on a busted rusty iron pole,
>   companion, we thought the same thoughts of the
>   soul, bleak and blue and sad-eyed, surrounded
>   by the gnarled steel roots of trees of machinery.
> The oily water on the river mirrored the red sky, sun
>   sank on top of final Frisco peaks. . .

"This actually happened"; as Kerouac tells it:[33]

"Had you been with me the other day sitting on the
littered banks of a San Francisco canal (little river
actually) by the banana boats and general warehouses
and churchhouses of commerciality, listening to Allen
Ginsberg the idealistic young poet from Paterson New
Jersey deliver a great sad sutra speech about a grime-
covered sunflower we found behind the billboards, dead,
gray, still, standing—"Ah Sunflower, weary of time"— .
. ."

Compare Ginsberg's poem with Kerouac himself, in "The
Railroad Earth":[39]

"There was a little alley in San Francisco back of the

Southern Pacific station at Third and Townsend in redbrick of drowsy lazy afternoons. . .

. . . you can see that sonofabitch red light waving Mars signal light waving in the dark big red markers blowing up and down and sending fires in the keenpure lostpurity lovelyskies of old California in the late sad night of autumn spring comefall winter's summertime tall, like trees. . .

So now it's purple in the sky, the whole rim America falling spilling over the west mountains into the eternal and orient sea, and there's your sad field and lovers twined and the wine is in the earth already and in Watsonville up ahead at the end of my grimy run. . ."

Ginsberg takes on Kerouac's setting, imagery, tone, outlook, and energy—"we thought the same thoughts"—rendering them with poetry's compression of syntax and music. He acknowledges this in his dedication, in which he praises Kerouac for "creating a spontaneous bop prosody. . . Several phrases and the title of *Howl* are taken from him."

He takes off from Walt Whitman's "Crossing Brooklyn Ferry",[60] on one shore,

What thought you have of me,

to make both apostrophe and homage to him,

What thoughts I have of you tonight, Walt Whitman,

in "A Supermarket in California," on the other shore. The book's epigraph is from "Song of Myself, 24":[60]

Unscrew the locks from the doors!
Unscrew the doors themselves from the jambs!

Once "the barriers" are "broken down," says M. L. Rosenthal, "the sophisticated intelligence must learn (with Whitman and

Blake, to accept sympathetically Ginsberg's identification with these figures) entirely new perspectives of human acceptance and value. That is one important aim, at least, of the revolutionary movement in poetry as it exists today."[65]

Inside the prophetic rage of "Howl" is a revolution of the politics of the nation, society, sexuality, toward liberation:

> who burned cigarette holes in their arms protesting the
>   narcotic tobacco haze of Capitalism,
> . . .
> who howled on their knees in the subway and were
>   dragged off the roof waving genitals and
>   manuscripts,
> . . .
> who copulated ecstatic and insatiate with a bottle of
>   beer a sweetheart a package of cigarettes a
>   candle and fell off the bed, and continued along
>   the floor. . .

Liberty, honesty, sensuality. Ginsberg's bare negations and implicit affirmations are voiced in an appropriate form, in a natural language, in this American classic.

4th Chorus:
Bomb:
Gregory Corso

Gregory Corso wrote early Beat poetry in *The Vestal Lady on Brattle*[66] and *Gasoline*,[67] the latter published by Ferlinghetti's City Lights with an introduction by Ginsberg, and including the poem, "Sun," which begins:

> Sun hypnotic! holy ball protracted long and sure! firey
> goblet! day-babble!
> Sun, sun-webbed heat! tropic goblet dry! spider thirst!
> Sun, unwater!
> Sun misery sun ire sun sick sun dead sun rot sun relic!
> Sun o'er Afric sky low and tipped, spilt, almost empty,
> hollow vial, sunbone, sunstone, iron sun,
> sundial.

In 1956 he came to San Francisco and continued in this line, working on a series of long odes, circular meditations on a single word: "Power," "Food," "Army," "Park." They share their one-

word titles and rhapsodic form with Ginsberg's "Howl"[55] and
Ferlinghetti's "HE".[2] In a letter to Ginsberg, he suggests "Power"
as the precursor to *Bomb*: ". . . Power is the germ of this. . ."[72]
Dedicated to Ginsberg, "Power"[69] is in the same vein formally:

> I resemble fifty miles of Power
> I cut my fingernails with a red Power
> In buses I stand on huge volumes of Spanish Power
> The girl I love is like a goat splashing golden cream
> Power

with the same tone:

> October you fat month of gloom and poetry
> It's no longer your melodious graveyard air
> Your night-headed cypresses
> Your lovely dead moon
> It is October of me! My Power!
> Alive with a joy a sparkle a laugh

But abstract "Power" becomes an intense real object in
Bomb. In these years, kids in school were taught duck and cover:
when sirens went off and a Russian thermonuclear bomb was
about to explode on them, they were to crouch under their little
wooden desks, with their arms sheltering their heads, until the
all clear sounded. At this point, protest against the politics of
fear began.

In interview, play, and letter, Corso remembered the origin
of *Bomb*:

> ". . . I saw the kids Ban the Bomb, Ban the Bomb, and I
> said, 'It's a death shot that's laid on them.'" ". . . it's not as
> if the Bomb had never fallen, so how am I going to tackle
> this thing, suddenly death was the big shot to handle,
> Gregory, not just the Bomb."[71] ". . . all the babies to come
> will have to ask what the shelters are, and the parents
> will have to explain to them, and not many parents can

explain death, so the poor kids will have to consult their deaths when everything about them is life."[70] ". . . Bomb, wrote it during mad period of this small attic great room overlooking Seine and medieval tower in which Marie Antoinette waited her head, and cone towers allwheres. Summer, on drugs, H and O, in this here room, with great global weeps about life I suddenly woke up to, and thus Bomb."[72]

The poem[69] was composed from 1957 to 1958. An early manuscript has on recto the poem in handwriting, and verso lines from a typescript, cut and pasted in the shape of a mushroom cloud:

BOMB

Budger of history Brake of time You Bomb
Toy of universe Grandest of all snatched-sky I cannot hate you
Do I hate the mischievous thunderbolt the jawbone of an ass
The bumpy club of One Million B.C. the mace the flail the axe
Catapult DaVinci tomahawk Cochise flintlock Kidd dagger Rathbone
Ah and the sad desperate gun of Verlaine Pushkin Dillinger Bogart
And hath not St. Michael a burning sword St. George a lance David a sling
Bomb you are as cruel as man makes you and you're no crueller than cancer
All man hates you they'd rather die by car-crash lightning drowning
Falling off a roof electric-chair heart-attack old age old age O Bomb
They'd rather die by anything but you Death's finger is free-lance
Not up to man whether you boom or not Death has long since distributed its
categorical blue I sing thee Bomb Death's extravagance Death's jubilee
Gem of Death's supremest blue The flyer will crash his death will differ
with the climber who'll fall To die by cobra is not to die by bad pork
Some die by swamp some by sea and some by the bushy-haired man in the night
O there are deaths like witches of Arc Scarey deaths like Boris Karloff
No-feeling deaths like birth-death sadless deaths like old pain Bowery
Abandoned deaths like Capital Punishment stately deaths like senators
And unthinkable deaths like Harpo Marx girls on Vogue covers my own
I do not know just how horrible Bombdeath is I can only imagine
Yet no other death I know has so laughable a preview I scope
a city New York City streaming starkeyed subway shelter
Scores and scores A fumble of humanity High heels bend
Hats whelming away Youth forgetting their combs
Ladies not knowing what to do with their shopping bags
Unperturbed gum machines Yet dangerous 3rd rail
Ritz Brothers from the Bronx caught in the A train
The smiling Schenley poster will always smile
Impish death Satyr Bomb Bombdeath
Turtles exploding over Istanbul
The jaguar's flying foot
soon to sink in arctic snow
Penguins plunged against the Sphinx
The top of the Empire State
arrowed in a broccoli field in Sicily
Eiffel shaped like a C in Magnolia Gardens
St. Sophia peeling over Sudan

Larry Beckett

O athletic Death   Sportive Bomb
the temples of ancient times
their grand ruin ceased
Electrons   Protons   Neutrons
gathering Hesperean hair
walking the dolorous gulf of Arcady
joining marble helmsmen
entering the final amphitheater
with a hymnody feeling of all Troys
heralding cypressean torches
racing plumes and banners
and yet knowing Homer with a step of grace
Lo the visiting team of Present
the home team of Past
Lyre and tuba together joined
Hark the hotdog soda olive grape
gala galaxy robed and uniformed
commissary   O the happy stands
Ethereal root and cheer and boo
The billioned all-time attendance
The Zeusian pandemonium
Hermes racing Owens
The Spitball of Buddha
Christ striking out
Luther stealing third
Planetarium Death   Hosannah Bomb
Gush the final rose   O Spring Bomb
Come with thy gown of dynamite green
unmenace Nature's inviolate eye
Before you the wimpled Past
behind you the hallooing Future   O Bomb
Bound in the grassy clarion air
like the fox of the tally-ho
thy field the universe thy hedge the geo
Leap Bomb   bound Bomb   frolic zig and zag
The stars a swarm of bees in thy binging bag
Stick angels on your jubilee feet
wheels of rainlight on your bunky seat
You are due and behold you are due

and the heavens are with you
hosanna incalescent glorious liaison
BOMB O havoc antiphony molten cleft BOOM
Bomb mark infinity a sudden furnace
spread thy multitudinous encompassed Sweep
set forth awful agenda
Carrion stars   charnel planets   carcass elements
Corpse the universe   tee-hee finger-in-the-mouth hop
over its long long dead Nor
From thy nimbled matted spastic eye
exhaust deluges of celestial ghouls
From thy appellational womb
spew birth-gusts of great worms
Rip open your belly Bomb
from your belly outflock vulturic salutations
Battle forth your spangled hyena finger stumps
along the brink of Paradise
O Bomb   O final Pied Piper
both sun and firefly behind your shock waltz
God abandoned mock-nude
beneath His thin false-talc'd apocalypse
He cannot hear thy flute's
happy-the-day profanations
He is spilled deaf into the Silencer's warty ear
His Kingdom an eternity of crude wax
Clogged clarions untrumpet Him
Sealed angels unsing Him
A thunderless God   A dead God
O Bomb   thy BOOM His tomb
That I lean forward on a desk of science
an astrologer dabbling in dragon prose
half-smart about wars   bombs   especially bombs
That I am unable to hate what is necessary to love
That I can't exist in a world that consents
a child in a park   a man dying in an electric-chair
That I am able to laugh at all things
all that I know and do not know   thus to conceal my pain
That I say I am a poet and therefore love all man
knowing my words to be the acquainted prophecy of all men

and my unwords no less an acquaintanceship
That I am manifold
a man pursuing the big lies of gold
or a poet roaming in bright ashes
or that which I imagine myself to be
a shark-toothed sleep   a man-eater of dreams
I need not then be all-smart about bombs
Happily so   for if I felt bombs were caterpillars
I'd doubt not they'd become butterflies
There is a hell for bombs
They're there   I see them there
They sit in bits and sing songs
mostly German songs
and two very long American songs
and they wish there were more songs
especially Russian and Chinese songs
and some more very long American songs
Poor little Bomb that'll never be
an Eskimo song   I love thee
I want to put a lollipop
in thy furcal mouth
A wig of Goldilocks on thy baldy bean
and have you skip with me Hansel and Gretel
along the Hollywoodian screen
O Bomb in which all lovely things
moral and physical anxiously participate
O fairylike plucked from the
grandest universe tree
O piece of heaven which gives
both mountain and anthill a sun
I am standing before your fantastic lily door
I bring you Midgardian roses   Arcadian musk
Reputed cosmetics from the girls of heaven
Welcome me   fear not thy opened door
nor thy cold ghost's grey memory
nor the pimps of indefinite weather
their cruel terrestrial thaw
Oppenheimer is seated
in the dark pocket of Light

Fermi is dry in Death's Mozambique
Einstein his mythmouth
a barnacled wreath on the moon-squid's head
Let me in   Bomb   rise from that pregnant-rat corner
nor fear the raised-broom nations of the world
O Bomb I love you
I want to kiss your clank   eat your boom
You are a paean   an acme of scream
a lyric hat of Mister Thunder
O resound thy tanky knees
BOOM   BOOM   BOOM   BOOM   BOOM
BOOM ye skies and BOOM ye suns
BOOM BOOM ye moons   ye stars BOOM
nights ye BOOM   ye days ye BOOM
BOOM BOOM ye winds   ye clouds ye rains
go BANG ye lakes   ye oceans BING
Barracuda BOOM and cougar BOOM
Ubangi BOOM   orangutang
BING BANG BONG BOOM   bee bear baboon
ye BANG ye BONG ye BING
the tail the fin the wing
Yes   Yes   into our midst a bomb will fall
Flowers will leap in joy their roots aching
Fields will kneel proud beneath the halleluyahs of the wind
Pinkbombs will blossom   Elkbombs will perk their ears
Ah many a bomb that day will awe the bird a gentle look
Yet   not enough to say a bomb will fall
or even contend celestial fire goes out
Know that the earth will madonna the Bomb
that in the hearts of men to come more bombs will be born
magisterial bombs wrapped in ermine   all beautiful
and they'll sit plunk on earth's grumpy empires
fierce with moustaches of gold

*

*   *

This poem, an ode by length, has an unusually wide reach of cultural reference, which is characteristic of Beat poetry, as in Ferlinghetti's allusions to Charlie Chaplin and James Joyce,[15] Kerouac's Zen and Crazy Horse,[38] and Ginsberg's Blake and jazz.[55] We find in the first seven lines of *Bomb* the thunder of Zeus and Thor, Samson's jawbone of an ass, the B-movie One Million B.C., and Leonardo Da Vinci, Cochise, Captain Kidd, Basil Rathbone, Paul Verlaine, Alexander Pushkin, John Dillinger, Humphrey Bogart, St. Michael, St. George, and David. This is not decorative but functional, as it not only details various deaths, but evokes the sensation that nuclear war anywhere involves the whole world. Later Oppenheimer, Fermi, and Einstein appear, whose science made the bomb possible. *Bomb* faces its overwhelming subject playfully: "Toy of universe, gum machines, Sportive Bomb, frolic zig and zag, tee-hee, Pied Piper, dabbling, lollipop, fairylike, tanky knees, ye oceans BING, Pinkbombs." In this poem, laughter is lifted against death, and this theme is conveyed by the playful tone.

Corso's intention was to print *Bomb* not on pages, or front and back of a broadside, but as one long page, like Kerouac's *On the Road* scroll; this has never been realized in print, though it should be said that when it's read online, readers scroll through it. Pattern poetry has a tradition going back before Greece, with Simias of Rhodes, to Persian calligraphy. *Bomb*, finished in Paris, may have had its mushroom cloud layout inspired by Guillaume Apollinaire's early 20th-century concrete poems *Calligrammes* (1916),[74] and George Herbert's 17th-century shape poems,[75] with centering making the image easy to read, and capitals for emphasis:

Beat Poetry

The Altar

A broken ALTAR, Lord thy servant rears,
Made of a heart, and cemented with teares:
Whose parts are as thy hand did frame;
No workmans tool hath touch'd the same
A HEART alone
Is such a stone,
As nothing but
Thy pow'r doth cut.
Wherefore each part
Of my hard heart
Meets in this frame,
To praise thy Name:
That if I chance to hold my peace,
These stones to praise thee may not cease.
O let thy blessed SACRIFICE be mine,
And sanctifie this ALTAR to be thine.

Bomb, though printed without breaks, is articulated into fourteen strophes: an introductory couplet followed by distinct stanzas varying between nine and twenty-five lines:

	Invocation: to Bomb
1-2	I cannot hate you
	Instance Bomb
3-20	O there are deaths
	Imagine Bomb
21-29	New York City
	Reconceive Bomb
30-38	Impish death
39-63	Sportive Bomb
64-76	Spring Bomb

There is an original music, as in:

> Electrons   Protons   Neutrons
> gathering Hesperean hair
> walking the dolorous gulf of Arcady
> joining marble helmsmen
> entering the final amphitheater
> with a hymnody feeling of all Troys
> heralding cypressean torches
> racing plumes and banners
> and yet knowing Homer with a step of grace

The suffixes repeat, –ons in the first line, and –ing in every other line: "gathering / walking / joining / entering / feeling / heralding / feeling / knowing"; and there is a chain of breath in "Hesperean / helmsmen / hymnody / heralding / Homer."

Its free verse lines are fused into a single line with gaps

between, to make a long line, or enjambed into the following line:

I do not know just how horrible Bombdeath is I can only imagine
    Yet no other death I know has so laughable a preview   I scope
    a city   New York City   streaming   starkeyed   subway shelter

It's free to riff on blank verse

> thy field the universe thy hedge the geo
> Leap Bomb   bound Bomb   frolic zig and zag
> The stars a swarm of bees in thy binging bag

or a tetrameter quatrain

> BOOM BOOM ye moons   ye stars BOOM
> nights ye BOOM   ye days ye BOOM
> BOOM BOOM ye winds   ye clouds ye rains
> go BANG ye lakes   ye oceans BING

The capitals / alliteration / onomatopoeia of "BING BANG BONG BOOM" power the stresses, and represent the bomb exploding.

The diction is as wide as the allusions. Words can be archaic: "Lo the visiting team, Hark the hotdog, Come with thy gown, BOOM ye skies." "Thy" and "thee" are used in the Romantic way of invoking the sacred, but are here subverted in referencing the weapon of annihilation. This language is side by side with the contemporary and colloquial: "home team, hotdog, root, boo." Corso is remarkably free with all kinds of coinings: "Budger, Bombdeath, billioned, geo, untrumpet, furcal, mythmouth, tanky." The musical gesture of introducing near-nonsense and nonsense words, Corso shares with Kerouac.

The poem is an apostrophe and a series of appositives:

> Budger of history   Brake of time   You   Bomb
> Toy of universe   Grandest of all snatched-sky   I cannot hate you

76

It's big enough to contain catalogs:

> Do I hate the mischievous thunderbolt   the jawbone of an ass
> The bumpy club of One Million B.C. the mace   the flail   the axe

a baseball game:

> The Spitball of Buddha
> Christ striking out

inventive metaphors:

> You are a paean   an acme of scream
> a lyric hat of Mister Thunder

and the explosion:

> BOOM   BOOM   BOOM   BOOM   BOOM
> BOOM ye skies and BOOM ye suns

The literary inspiration for the object of this poem may have come from Ginsberg's "Howl":[55]

> monstrous bombs!
> . . .
> our own souls' airplanes roaring over the roof they've
> come to drop angelic bombs

and one of "Howl's" inspirations, William Carlos Williams' "Asphodel, That Greeny Flower" (1955):[63]

> I am reminded
> that the bomb
> also
> is a flower
> dedicated
> howbeit
> to our destruction.

The mere picture
of the exploding bomb

and Guillaume Apollinaire, again, in his long poem "Zone"[76] (1913), translated in an essential anthology in 1958 by Dudley Fitts, and beginning like *Bomb* with an apotheosis:

After all you are weary of this oldtime world

Shepherdess O Eiffel Tower your flock of bridges is
bleating this morning

with a fresh tone, bringing the machine into poetry, in proto-surrealistic imagery:

Christ who climbs the sky better than any aviator
He holds the world record for altitude
Pupil Christ of the eye
. . .
The angels flash around the pretty tightroper
Icarus Enoch Elijah Apollonius of Tyana
Bob about this first airplane

A major model is Percy Shelley, invoked in "I Held a Shelley Manuscript," which shares the word "cypressean" with *Bomb*. The major earlier Corso poem "Ode to Coit Tower" alludes to "Ode to the West Wind" (1820),[77] which is an apostrophe and a series of appositives addressed to a destructive force:

O wild West Wind, thou breath of Autumn's being,
. . .
Wild Spirit, which art moving everywhere;
Destroyer and Preserver: Hear, oh, hear!

In its climax, the poet identifies himself with destruction, while breaking through to an understanding that it is also a force of renewal:

> Be thou, Spirit fierce,
> My spirit! be thou me, impetuous one!
> Drive my dead thoughts over the universe
> Like wither'd leaves to quicken a new birth;

His identification magnifies his speech:

> . . . my words among mankind!
> Be through my lips to unawaken'd earth
> The trumpet of a prophecy!

Corso sees its humor linking *Bomb* to "Howl": ". . .politics and betterment of earthly conditions is death to poetry, unless these newspaper subjects be treated with light, love and laughter, like Allen's Howl and my Bomb."[72]

Bomb begins with the poet invoking and accepting the bomb as a way of dying, neither more nor less than other deaths. He imagines it exploding over New York, then reconceives it as play, imposing his own joy on the weapon of destruction. But this is retracted as he broods on its actual consequences: the deaths of man and God. But he reasserts himself: "That I am able to laugh at all things" and so transcend them; this intensifies into love, in a Shelleyan gesture of communion. He's said of the poem, "its content is one of love, love for life, love for man— and the only way for me to do this was not to say 'O Bomb how terrible you are,' but to say 'O Bomb I love you.'"[72] The poet, facing politicians who out of fear and hatred are poised to atomize him, shows the poverty of their values by returning love and acceptance. As Ginsberg said, "it just reduces the bomb to insignificance because the poem is greater than the bomb." In a heroic moment, he invites the bomb to go off; he can celebrate and so defeat it. *Bomb* ends like "Ode to the West Wind," facing the future. It warns that this is not the end; more bombs will come for him to face, "knowing my words to be the acquainted prophecy of all men."

In Kerouac's phrase, beat is "down and out but full of

intense conviction."[34] This poem embodies that, with its honesty in acknowledging himself as a victim of terror and maybe extinction, its passion in invalidating those threatening him, out of the superflux of his heart:

Welcome me   fear not thy opened door

In the age of nuclear warfare, it is literally as if the governments had contrived to aim a gun at our heads. While established poets went on writing villanelles about time, Corso had the awareness and courage to turn and speak to the gunman, face to face.

In 1958, Ferlinghetti published *Bomb* as a broadside. The following year, Corso assembled a book of his one-word-title odes for him: "Title is STARMEAT. Poems will be in chronological order: Power, Food, Army, Park, Bomb, Marriage, Police, Xmas, Death, Hair. That makes ten mad mad poems in all for next book. . ."[72] In the first critical book devoted to Corso, Gregory Stephenson calls these poems "babble and bombast against all the various agencies that debase the human spirit and impair true life . . . The poems are less meditations or discourses upon their themes than they are imaginative explorations, proceeding by associative leaps and oblique correspondences, by expansions and fusions and transformations."[79] But Ferlinghetti rejected the manuscript, which, extended by a number of lyrics, was published in 1960 by New Directions, who had published Ferlinghetti's *A Coney Island of the Mind*.

Equivocal about the title, *The Happy Birthday of Death*, Corso wrote an unacknowledged poem[69] listing other options, to be put opposite the title page, with an arrow from the winner to the title, which traces the vein of absurdity from life to art to this book, and perfectly embodies the Beat ethos:

Larry Beckett

SALEABLE TITLES

Fried Shoes
Pipe Butter
Radiator Soup
Flash Gordon soap
Areopagus
Remarkable
Caesarean operation
Sterile Tunisia
Ashes
Cars are love
Earth is not even a star
Fearful compassion
A trembling of roses
Woe is me!
Coffee
Gargoyle liver
Jellies
Of all substances St Michael is the stickiest
Hairy abdomen
General indifference futilely thrown
Watermelon
The Deserted Desert
The Wet Sea
The Rumpled Backyard
Agamemnon
Treelight
The Happy Birthday of Death
Wrought reckless luke mood
All is permissible
A king is a very strange thing
Hail, Jack Falstaff!

As in *Bomb*, the references range from pop to classic culture, from Flash Gordon, the 1930s comic strip, to Areopagus, the hill and court in ancient Athens.

The poem immediately preceding *Bomb* in the book, with a completely different kind of excellence, is "Marriage",[69] beginning with rhymes, rare in Beat poetry, in long free lines:

> Should I get married? Should I be good?
> Astound the girl next door with my velvet suit and
>   faustus hood?
> Don't take her to movies but to cemeteries
> tell all about werewolf bathtubs and forked clarinets
> then desire her and kiss her and all the preliminaries
> and she going just so far and I understanding why
> not getting angry saying You must feel! It's beautiful to
>   feel!
> Instead take her in my arms lean against an old crooked
>   tombstone
> and woo her the entire night the constellations in the
>   sky —

He uses mock surrealist images, "Flash Gordon soap," "Radio belly," "Radiant brains," as emblems of poetry, of his variance from the mainstream culture, "hanging a picture of Rimbaud on the lawnmower," which is at once painful and comic:

> asking me Do you take this woman for your lawful
>   wedded wife?
> And I trembling what to say say Pie Glue!

This theme is adumbrated in "Food":[69]

> Wisconsin provisions
> Insufficient when I have absolute dairy visions:
> Corduroy eggs, owl cheese, pipe butter,

Kerouac had read the manuscript, and the year after the poems were written, the year before they were published, in his ad-libbed narration for the Robert Frank / Alfred Leslie film, *Pull My Daisy* (1961), loosely based on Act 3 of his play *Beat*

Generation, he improvised on the theme, as poets invade the household:[42]

> "Gregory Corso and Allen Ginsberg there, laying their beer cans out on the table, bringing up all the wine, wearing hoods and parkas, falling on the couch, all bursting with poetry while she's saying, Now you get your coat, get your little hat and we're going to go off to school."

They use similar gestures: "magic beer bottle," "silver ladder," "Is baseball holy?" and Corso is invoked with the second line of Saleable Titles: "Poor Gregory, the hero of stove and pipe butter."

Bomb is included in *The Happy Birthday of Death* in its broadside form, as a fold-out, making the book unique. Corso said, "ye BANG ye BONG ye BING. There's a lot of interplay in that poem. When it's read, it's a sound poem."[71] He recorded it in 1959 at the Library of Congress; music was overlaid in 2002.[73] In the following decade, writing to Ginsberg, he saw the book's unity: "*Happy Birthday of Death*, of bombs, cars are real, of fear of death, of ambitious attempt to poetize in turn subjectize death, yet of humor, of lost hair death, and marriageless death."[72]

The poet Dom Moraes says, "More than any other modern poet, he's put the lyre back into the lyric, illuminating the haphazard mosaic cast by his thoroughgoing imagination of Bomb—the 'Budger of history.'"[78] This book of true odes and lyrics is an essential Beat text.

Beat Poetry

5th Chorus:

Hotel:

John Wieners / Michael
McClure / Philip Lamantia

John Wieners couldn't avoid renaissances. After overhearing Charles Olson read his poetry, then reading through the *Black Mountain Review*, edited by Robert Creeley, and studying with them at the avant garde college of the same name, he was considered one of the poets in the Boston Renaissance. The day his review *Measure* was first published, he was fired from Harvard University's Lamont Library, drove west, and found himself among the poets of the San Francisco Renaissance.

Though Olson's "projective verse" and "composition by field" add up to nothing more than writing free verse while thinking about breathing, they inspired Wieners. He wrote in his journal, "These days shall be my poems. . . Sur-real is the only way to endure the real we find heaped up in our cities."[84] Over nine days, in a flophouse in the red-light district, he wrote *The Hotel Wentley Poems*.[80]

A poem for vipers

I sit in Lees. At 11:40 PM with
Jimmy the pusher. He teaches me
Ju Ju. Hot on the table before us
shrimp foo yong, rice and mushroom
chow yuke. Up the street under the wheels
of a strange car is his stash — The ritual.
We make it. And have made it.
For months now together after midnight.
Soon I know the fuzz will
interrupt, will arrest Jimmy and
I shall be placed on probation. The poem
does not lie to us. We lie under
its law, alive in the glamour of this hour
able to enter into the sacred places
of his dark people, who carry secrets
glassed in their eyes and hide words
under the coats of their tongue.

6.16.58

This poem relates a connection, where a drug user and a drug salesman do business, in Lee's, a Chinese restaurant not far from the Hotel Wentley. It's a short lyric, written in compact free verse lines, varying between six and thirteen syllables, but gravitating toward blank verse, with an insistent alliteration: "Jimmy / Ju Ju, street / strange / stash, make / made / months / midnight, lie / lie / law / alive, sacred / secrets." It's laced with the argot of illegal drugs, the privacy of the language evoking the secrecy necessary in breaking the law: "viper": marijuana smoker; "pusher": drug salesman; "stash": hidden supply; "fuzz": police.

The poem follows an arc from precise fact, "I sit in Lees. At 11:40 PM," to classic figure, "We lie under / its law," to surreal image, "who carry secrets / glassed in their eyes."

There is no trace of the styles of Olson or Creeley here. "A poem for vipers" is a contemporary version of the Romantic lyric, as defined by M. H. Abrams:

"They present a determinate speaker in a particularized, and usually a localized, outdoor setting, whom we overhear as he carries on, in a fluent vernacular which rises easily to a more formal speech, a sustained colloquy, sometimes with himself or with the outer scene, but more frequently with a silent human auditor, present or absent. The speaker begins with a description of the landscape; an aspect or change of aspect in the landscape evokes a varied but integral process of memory, thought, anticipation, and feeling which remains closely intervolved with the outer scene. In the course of this meditation the lyric speaker achieves an insight, faces up to a tragic loss, comes to a moral decision, or resolves an emotional problem. Often the poem rounds upon itself to end where it began, at the outer scene, but with an altered mood and deepened understanding which is the result of the intervening meditation."[85]

A model for this kind of poem is this near sonnet, by Samuel Coleridge:[86]

Work Without Hope

Lines composed 21st February 1825

All Nature seems at work. Slugs leave their lair—
The bees are stirring—birds are on the wing—
And WINTER slumbering in the open air,
Wears on his smiling face a dream of Spring!
And I, the while, the sole unbusy thing,
Nor honey make, nor pair, nor build, nor sing.

       Yet well I ken the banks where amaranths blow,
Have traced the fount whence streams of nectar flow.
Bloom, O ye amaranths! bloom for whom ye may,
For me ye bloom not! Glide, rich streams, away!
With lips unbrighten'd, wreathless brow, I stroll:
And would you learn the spells that drowse my soul?
WORK WITHOUT HOPE draws nectar in a sieve,
And HOPE without an OBJECT cannot live.

The two poems, besides being strong examples of the Romantic lyric, have strange parallels: in both, drugs figure, as "the spells" are from laudanum, and the exact date of composition is noted.

In "A poem for vipers," after the pure fact, the restaurant, the hour, his companion, the dinner, ambiguity is built on simple words: "We make it" can be "we transact a sale" or "we have sex"; this is maintained in "together after midnight" and "the glamour of this hour," as love is reduced to need. He anticipates the interruption, not the end, of this relationship, by the law, and this leads him to intensify his near religious connection to this counterculture, the ritual, the dark people and their sacred places, the secrets in their glassy eyes, the words hiding under their coated tongues.

Wieners has taken the Romantic lyric indoors, in the city, in a poem so naked it confesses a crime and could be used in evidence against him. In a subculture dedicated to hiding from the law, he tells the truth, and names the drug dealer, the place and time where the deal goes down, and the location of the stash, as he celebrates another law, of poetry, another kind of lying, under honesty: "The poem / does not lie to us. We lie under / its law." This poem acts out Kerouac's definition of Beat, "down and out but full of intense conviction."[34]

This honesty extends to acknowledging the poem as artifice: The poem states "The poem," the titles of the poems in the book are "A poem for record players," "A poem for vipers," "A poem for painters," and so on, and the title of the book is *The Hotel Wentley Poems*. The book was published in 1958 by Auerhahn Press, who also published McClure's *Hymns to St. Geryon and Other Poems* and *Dark Brown*, and Lamantia's *Ekstasis*. It was reissued in a revised edition in 1965 by the owner of that press as *The Hotel Wentley Poems: Original Versions*,[81] in which John Wieners tries to get even closer to his original vision. "A poem for vipers" was unchanged. Two of the eight poems were recorded in 1959 at the Mad Monster Mammoth Poets' Reading.[83]

In a contemporary poem, Frank O'Hara alludes to the book: "everybody here is running around after dull pleasantries and / wondering if *The Hotel Wentley Poems* is as great as I say it is..."[87] Ginsberg wrote the Foreword to Wieners' *Selected Poems*, saying "John Wieners's glory is solitary, as pure poet—a man reduced to loneness in poetry, without worldly distractions—and a man become one with his poetry."[82] The Beat biographer Neeli Cherkovski says, "*Wentley* is an implosion, a spiritual journey into the body and mind, the opposite of the explosive, outward-flowing work of Wieners' contemporaries."[88] Working without Ferlinghetti's visuals, Kerouac's improvisations, Ginsberg's scale, or Corso's flamboyance, John Wieners writes in a true lyric voice, extending a tradition with sheer honesty. Robert Creeley sums this up: "His poems had nothing else in mind but their own fact."[89]

After working through free verse, Michael McClure swayed toward forms: "I was writing poems in the manner of Blake. A cross between Blake and Baudelaire, and at the same time learning forms like the Petrarchan sonnet, the ballad, the villanelle, the sestina."[7] When he saw Abstract Expressionist paintings, he started painting so that those gestures would move into his poetry: "They were learning to write their biographies in the movements of their body on a canvas."[7] He moved to San Francisco hoping to study with Clifford Still and Mark Rothko. They were gone, but he studied poetry with Robert Duncan, the one-time Black Mountain teacher, who discouraged his sonnets. Because his wife was about to give birth, he asked Ginsberg to organize the pivotal 6 Gallery reading, at which he recited his answer to Antonin Artaud, "Point Lobos: Animism," and the deconstructed ballad "For the Death of 100 Whales."[64]

He edited the magazine *Ark II / Moby I*, and published two books of poetry, *Passages* and *For Artaud*, and then wrote *Hymns to St. Geryon & Other Poems*.[90] He said, "I decided I should be what is represented there. Each one is like a very narrow vibration of what I am doing at a given time—what I felt was the most appropriate vibration."[7]

Larry Beckett

A NIGHT IN TUNISIA

The body does not change, — love moves
to meet the need.

That I am sick is not half of it.

I lie to tell you love
and the muscles knot in it
tying themselves that way
making ease.
Yes, and it is black inside me.
(which is not news)
Looking at your emptiness,

knowing it as the muscles change it.

"A Night in Tunisia" is Dizzy Gillespie's sinuous jazz song, a bop classic, released as a 78 single in 1946, best heard in his Town Hall concert with Charlie Parker the previous June. Ginsberg notes the power of this song over Kerouac: "Kerouac learned his line from—directly from Charlie Parker, and Gillespie, and Monk. He was listening in '43 to Symphony Sid and listening to 'Night in Tunisia' and all the Bird-flight-noted things which he then adapted to prose line."[94] McClure was listening to the same radio: "I went through all of those: Gillespie, Parker, 'Salt Peanuts,' 'A Night in Tunisia. . .' I listened to the music for a year before touching it. Before it even got through my skin."[7]

McClure's brief lyric, "A Night in Tunisia", is a love / sex poem. It's rendered abstractly, without narrative or description, in wide words: the man is "muscles," and the woman "emptiness." Like Corso's *Bomb*, it's centered on the page, but where that was meant to shape the cloud, this is, again, abstract. It moves the ritual left margin to a center axis, and the poem takes on bilateral symmetry, like the body. The punctuation marks make shorter pauses, and the spaces longer. The lines vary continuously in syllables, but are anchored to the center; there are no figures but words natural to the body: "lie, knot"; everything is literal: there is a tension between the loose music and the tight array, between the abstract language and the concrete encounter.

The words are general but bodily: "body, love, moves, sick, muscles, ease, black, emptiness, change." McClure's poetry and aesthetics are anchored in physicality. He describes listening to "A Night in Tunisia" as "touching it," as getting it "through my skin." In the preface to *Hymns to St. Geryon*, he writes, ". . . I want a writing of the Emotions, intellect and physiology. The direct emotional statement from the body (from the organs and from the energy of movements). . . A poem is as much of me as an arm." And, in one of the hymns, "I am the body, the animal, the poem / is a gesture of mine."[90]

McClure's major influence is William Blake. He said, "As for Blake, I used to dream I was Blake!"[7] And, after a conversation with Ginsberg: "Allen has a Blake who is a Blake of prophecy, a Blake who speaks out against the dark Satanic Mills. My Blake is a Blake of body and of vision."[4] Blake's sexual testament is *Visions of the Daughters of Albion* (1793), who sigh "towards America":[95]

> I cry, Love! Love! Love! happy happy Love! free as the
>   mountain wind!
> Can that be Love, that drinks another as a sponge drinks
>   water?
> That clouds with jealousy his nights, with weepings all
>   the day:
> To spin a web of age around him, grey and hoary! dark!
> Till his eyes sicken at the fruit that hangs before his
>   sight.
> Such is self-love that envies all! a creeping skeleton
> With lamplike eyes watching around the frozen
>   marriage bed.
>
> But silken nets and traps of adamant will Oothoon
>   spread,
> And catch for thee girls of mild silver, or of furious
>   gold:
> I'll lie beside thee on a bank & view their wanton play
> In lovely copulation bliss on bliss with Theotormon. . .

In line with this, McClure said, "The prime purpose of my writing is liberation."[90] McClure's poem is not so much modeled after Blake's as it proceeds from it. A phrase from this poem, "for every thing that lives is holy," repeated elsewhere in Blake, inspired Ginsberg's "Footnote to Howl."[55]

"A Night in Tunisia's" few words are multivalent. It says the body doesn't change, it's full of desire; but "emptiness" is her sex, her body, and "the muscles change it," to fulfillment, so that there's a tension between statement and refutation. Love, moving to meet the need, is love as we understand it. But, after acknowledging being sick, with love, or repression, as in Blake, where "eyes sicken," he says "I lie to tell you love": in this, the sense of "I lie down with you to express my love" is subverted by that of "I speak false, and seduce with lies." Sickness is disease, but his muscles are "making ease." The "black inside" is the interior of his body, its mystery, and knowing it, he knows her womb, her emptiness, and love has moved to meet the need, of sex, and connection. The tensions in the music and contradiction, the swing of meanings, make this, like the action paintings of the Abstract Expressionist Franz Kline, a poem as gesture.

McClure was conscious of being in the Beat Generation, which he saw as "a spiritual occasion."[7] He collected the two poems read at the 6 Gallery with this poem, the more surreal broadside *Peyote Poem*, and several others, in *Hymns to St. Geryon and Other Poems*, an allusion to Dante's "Inferno" Canto XVII, where Geryon is a monster with wings, face of a just man, body of a serpent, tail of a scorpion, at the cliff before the circles of fraud:[96]

Behold him who infecteth all the world.

The title is sarcastic and honest at the same time, because McClure notes, "He seemed to be my patron. I had a luminous handsome face and a rather gross and flabby body. I felt that I was a kind of living hypocrisy or fraud."[97] McClure returns to the body.

"A Night in Tunisia" is grouped with the "Hymns to St. Geryon", but looks forward to *Dark Brown*,[91] McClure's own sexual testament, and a major effort, not to allude to sex using its language, as in Ginsberg's "Howl," but to write directly about the act, as a sacrament. In *Big Sur*, Kerouac calls it "The most fantastic poem in America. . ."[41] It was extended with "Fuck Ode" and the even more explicit lyric, "A Garland," without precedent in literature, poems which puritans would call worthless, but which are worthy. The two books were published together, making another composite Beat poetry text, in 1969,[92] and reprinted in 1980,[93] with the preface "From a Journal." A fragment of *Dark Brown* was recorded at the Mad Monster Mammoth Poets' Reading in 1963.[83]

Ginsberg introduced him by saying, "McClure's poetry

is a blob of protoplasmic energy."[98] Robert Creeley sees his physicality as well: ". . . I think his persistent involvement with meat package context of persons is to figure the instruction and wherewithal to bring by-product mind-thought abstractions back home to initial flesh and blood."[99] The critic Gregory Stephenson sums up in this way: "Beginning with the apparent contradictions of mind and body—mysticism and materialism, spirituality and sensuality, atavism and transcendence, human and nonhuman, energy and structure—the poet forges a new harmony and wholeness. . ."[97] Stephenson is referencing Thomas Aquinas as translated by James Joyce, who defined beauty as the coincidence of three values: wholeness and harmony; and to these, for McClure, add radiance.

Like McClure, Philip Lamantia was inspired in his poetry by painting, specifically, that of the surrealists Salvador Dali and Joan Miró. Shaped by his contacts with the French poet and aesthetician André Breton in New York, and the poet and anarchist Kenneth Rexroth in San Francisco, he published his first book, *Erotic Poems*, in 1946. Ferlinghetti points out, "He was the primary transmitter of French Surrealist poetry in this country. He was writing stream-of-consciousness Surrealist poetry, and he had a huge influence on Allen Ginsberg. Before that, Ginsberg was writing rather conventional poetry. It was Philip who turned him on to Surrealist writing. Then Ginsberg wrote 'Howl.'"[103] In that poem, the line

> who bared their brains to Heaven under the El and saw
> Mohammedan angels staggering on tenement
> roofs illuminated,

was inspired by a religious experience, which Lamantia told to Kerouac, who told Ginsberg:

"1953, Spring, aged 25, reading the Koran on a couch, one night, I was suddenly physically laid out by a powerful force beyond my volition, which rendered me almost comatose: suddenly, consciousness was contracted to a single point at the top of my head through which I was 'siphoned' beyond the room, space and time into another state of awareness that seemed utterly beyond any other state before or since experienced. I floated toward an endless-looking universe of misty, lighted color forms: green, red, blue and silver, which circulated before me companied by such bliss that the one dominant thought was: This is it; I never want to return to anywhere but this place—i.e., I wanted to remain in this Ineffable Blissful Realm and explore it forever—since I felt a radiance beyond even further within it and so, suddenly the outline of a benign bearded Face appeared to whom I addressed my desire to remain in this marvel—and who calmly replied: 'You can return, after you complete your work.'"[54]

In interviews, Lamantia has outlined his association of the religious with the aesthetic:

"Surrealism begins with the sacred. And the premise that each individual poet, or painter, seek the 'golden fleece' on his own."[104] "I wrote much of *Ekstasis*[100] during my initial conversion to Catholicism, in the early fifties, though I eventually drifted away from the Church. I didn't quite have the philosophical sophistication I have now, in terms of understanding mysticism. By 'mystic,' I mean the experience of having something previously unknown reveal itself to you, a direct communication with God. One in which you feel God's love in an ecstatic, physical way. . . In *Ekstasis*, I wrote 'Christ IS the marvellous!' so yes, I felt a continuity between surrealism and mysticism. I believe that erotic love and spiritual love are essentially the same. Take the word 'passion'; it indicates both the saint's experience of God and the lover's experience of the beloved, and with good reason."[105]

Beat Poetry

There is this distance between me and what I see

There is this distance between me and what I see
everywhere immanence of the presence of God
no more ekstasis
a cool head
watch watch watch
I'm here
He's over there . . . It's an Ocean . . .
sometimes I can't think of it, I fail, fail
There IS this look of love
there IS the tower of David
there IS the throne of Wisdom
there IS this silent look of love
Constant flight in air of the Holy Ghost
I long for the luminous darkness of God
I long for the superessential light of this darkness
another darkness I long for the end of longing
I long for the
              it is Nameless what I long for
a spoken word caught in its own meat saying nothing
This nothing ravishes beyond ravishing
There IS this look of love Throne Silent look of love

This is a classic visionary poem, asserting current distance from the divine, but its reality and bliss. It has a biblical air, with its repetitions and allusions to David and the Holy Ghost. It should be noted that the original title, Still Poem 9, has been stripped away; ekstasis, the title of the book in which the poem appears, is the Greek root of ecstasy, and means "being taken out of your senses," or transport; when Lamantia collected this in his *Selected Poems*[101] for City Lights, he put it in a section called "Trance Ports"; the tower of David is a citadel in Jerusalem, though a general sacred air is all this phrase intends.

The form is pure free verse, each line's syllables generated by statement and no other paradigm, though this is intensified by incantation, in repetition of word and phrase: "there is," appearing seven times including the title; "God" twice; "watch watch watch"; "fail, fail"; "look of love" four times; "throne" twice; "I long for" five times; "silent" twice; "darkness" three times; "nothing / This nothing"; "ravishes beyond ravishing"; while the emphatic upper case "IS" strengthens the rhythm. The imagery is natural: his head is "cool," "flight in air," "word caught in its own meat"; "the throne of Wisdom," however the reader imagines it, imposes itself in the last line, in the fragment "Throne."

Lamantia said, "I figure it was Blake and Poe who led me directly into Surrealism."[104] The mystic, not in ecstasy, not in communion with God, longs for their return, in images of light and love, as in the opening to William Blake's *Jerusalem* (1820):[106]

I am not a God afar off, I am a brother and friend:

The center of the poem may recall lines in Blake's "The Smile" (1803):[107]

There is a Smile of Love
And there is a Smile of Deceit
And there is a Smile of Smiles
In which these two Smiles meet

And when this mystic poem uses the word "ravishes," it sends us to an unacknowledged model, where erotic and spiritual love merge, John Donne's Holy Sonnet, "Batter my heart, three person'd God; for, you" (1609):[108]

Nor ever chast, except you ravish mee.

Lamantia describes composition, "This amounts to writing from and experiencing from a sort of waking trance state, a place from which many of the world's great prophetic writings have come—writings of the old biblical prophets, *The Song of Songs*, and so forth."[104] This poem, in essence, derives from the Psalms, as this for example, in the Revised Standard Version, which collocates David, tower, throne, love, with the longing for God:[109]

Psalm 61

To the choirmaster: with stringed instruments. A Psalm
        of David.

Hear my cry, O God,
listen to my prayer;
from the end of the earth I call to thee,
when my heart is faint.

Lead thou me
to the rock that is higher than I;
for thou art my refuge,
a strong tower against the enemy.

Let me dwell in thy tent for ever!
Oh to be safe under the shelter of thy wings!   *Selah*
For thou, O God, hast heard my vows,
thou hast given me the heritage of those who fear thy
        name.

Prolong the life of the king;
may his years endure to all generations!
May he be enthroned for ever before God;
bid steadfast love and faithfulness watch over him!

So will I ever sing praises to thy name,
as I pay my vows day after day.

Lamantia's poem is after ekstasis, watching the distance, longing for communion, and affirming, despite the distance, the look of love, tower of David, throne of wisdom. The Holy Ghost is hard to meet, in constant flight; he has to look into the oxymoronic luminous darkness for the superessential light. At the most dramatic point of this quest, words fail: "I long for the", and he acknowledges that it cannot be named. The look of love, which ravishes him, is erotic and spiritual at once.

Lamantia connects this state of mind with Kerouac's sense of Beat: "For me, my life between 1948 and 1952 was a kind of descent into the underworld, marked by the necessity to buy marijuana and other illicit medicines from the actual criminal underworld. Nevertheless, an abiding religious sense was always present among many of us—pot-oriented contemplative experiences, for the most part, and this is why Kerouac turned the meaning of 'beat' into 'beatific.'"[7]

At the 6 Gallery reading that launched Beat poetry, he read not his own, but work by another poet, in his memory. He refused to be included in the watershed "San Francisco Scene" issue of *Evergreen Review*. He was part of the Jazz/Poetry Trio, with Jack Kerouac, Howard Hart, and David Amram; in 1957, they gave the first poetry/jazz reading in New York, at the Brata Art Gallery. Two of his poems were recorded at the Mad Monster Mammoth Poets' Reading,[83] which he organized in 1959.

His own book of sacred poems came out that year, named *Ekstasis* after a word in this poem, and published by Auerhahn. The author's note says his poetry is "erotic, mythic, magical and devotional."[100] Its first poem is in the shape of a cross; it may have been inspired by George Herbert's shape poems on holy themes,[75] which may also have inspired Corso's *Bomb*. "In Fragments from an Aeroplane",[100] he writes:

> I'm here alone
> Where is HE, God of the PSALMS?

pointing to the theme and source of *There is this distance between me and what I see.*

Garrett Caples says, "While these works do share in the 'Beat' use of colloquial speech and hipster jargon, they retain 'the touch of the marvelous' Lamantia received from surrealism during his youth."[105] Neeli Cherkovski adds, ". . . Lamantia fixed more on the power of language, unrestrained by strict linear thinking."[88] Ginsberg calls Philip Lamantia "an American original, soothsayer even as Poe, genius in the language of Whitman, native companion and teacher to myself."[102]

When Ginsberg taught the Literary History of the Beat Generation, at the Naropa Institute in 1977, he included in Celestial Homework,[110] the reading list, Weiners' *The Hotel Wentley Poems*, McClure's "Fuck Ode" and "Garland" from *Dark Brown*, and Lamantia's *There is this distance between me and what I see* .

6th Chorus:
Riprap:
Gary Snyder / Philip Whalen / Lew Welch

Gary Snyder wrote poetry for ten years, abandoned it, and only then achieved the poems in his first book, *Riprap*:

> "I started writing poems when I was fifteen. I wrote ten years of poetry before *Riprap*. Phase one romantic teenage poetry about girls and mountains. . . And then phase two, college. Poems that echoed Yeats, Eliot, Pound, Williams, and Stevens. A whole five years of doing finger exercises in the modes of the various twentieth-century masters. All of that I scrapped; only a few traces of that even survive. I threw most of them in a burning barrel when I was about twenty-five. . ."[6]

> "I got interested in trying to study Zen first hand. Sort of broke off my anthropology career. . . I was enrolled, and had a fellowship in Indiana University. . . I just quit

mid-stream and said, 'I'm going out to Berkeley and study Chinese.' Took the Greyhound bus and went back to the West Coast. Got into the East Asian languages department. Also took some literature courses. And that's when I started reading Han Shan's texts. In the summer of '55 I started writing some more poems while I was up on trail crew. . ."[7]

"So when I wrote the first poems in *Riprap* it was after I had given up poetry. I went to work in the mountains in the summer of 1955 for the U. S. Park Service as a trail crew laborer and had already started classical Chinese study. I thought I had renounced poetry. Then I got out there and started writing these poems about the rocks and blue jays. I looked at them. They didn't look like any poems that I had ever written before. So I said, these must be my own poems. I date my work as a poet from the poems in *Riprap*."[6]

In the Yosemite wilderness, he wrote its opening poem:[111]

Larry Beckett

Mid-August at Sourdough Mountain Lookout

Down valley a smoke haze
Three days heat, after five days rain
Pitch glows on the fir-cones
Across rocks and meadows
Swarms of new flies.

I cannot remember things I once read
A few friends, but they are in cities.
Drinking cold snow-water from a tin cup
Looking down for miles
Through high still air.

This is direct notation of nature and mind. It captures, as closely as any poem, how it feels to live. In its title, "Sourdough Mountain", the location, in the Cascade Range in Washington, but which could be anywhere, is less consequential than "Lookout": the poet is a firewatch. In 1952, Snyder worked at that summer job at Crater Mountain, and in 1953, at Sourdough Mountain, inspiring this poem. In 1953, Phil Whalen worked at Sauk Mountain, and in 1954 and 1955, at Sourdough Mountain; he then wrote the poem "Sourdough Mountain Lookout," in *Like I Say*.[117] In 1956, Kerouac worked at Desolation Peak, and then wrote the essay "Alone on a Mountaintop," in *Lonesome Traveler*,[39] and the novel *Desolation Angels*.[40] Snyder included him in "Migration of Birds": "Jack Kerouac outside, behind my back / Reads the *Diamond Sutra* in the sun."[111] Kerouac portrayed all these poets: Snyder as Japhy Ryder and Whalen as Warren Coughlin in *The Dharma Bums*,[30] and Welch as Dave Wain in *Big Sur*.[41]

The poem's mode is telegraphic brevity: "Down valley a smoke haze"; but the line is free to expand into blank verse: "I cannot remember things I once read." Its lines, varying between four and ten syllables, occur in sets of five, as free verse stanzas. There are no figures; this concentrates attention on what language there is, as it wavers between heat, in "smoke, heat, glows," and cold, in "rain, cold snow-water, high still air." This concentration works for the music as well, with assonance edging into internal rhyme, in the same words: "haze / days / days / rain; glows / cones / cold / snow; miles / high." The language is bare, and though the words look ordinary, there are unusual compounds built up from them: "fir-cones, snow-water." The commas mark pauses, the periods turns of subject.

His acknowledged model is the Chinese poet Han Shan, from the T'ang dynasty, best read in his own translation, *Cold Mountain Poems*:[114]

3

In the mountains it's cold.

Always been cold, not just this year.
Jagged scarps forever snowed in
Woods in the dark ravines spitting mist.
Grass is still sprouting at the end of June.
Leaves begin to fall in early August.
And here am I, high on mountains,
Peering and peering, but I can't even see the sky.

Between Han Shan and Gary Snyder, there are "mountains /
mountain, cold / cold, year / days, scarps / rocks and meadows,
snowed in / snow-water, woods / fir-cones, mist / haze, grass
still sprouting / new flies, early August / Mid-August, high / for
miles, peering / looking down, see the sky / high still air." There
is the same bare statement. After observation of the mountains,
the poet appears towards the end. Snyder's references to reading
and forgetting, friends and separation, may have been suggested
by another Han Shan poem, 5:[112]

. . . a grey-haired man
Mumbles along reading Huang and Lao.
For ten years I haven't gone back home
I've even forgotten the way by which I came.

The influence of Chinese poetry is mediated by his encounter
with William Carlos Williams, who recited at Reed College in
1950, insisted on "No ideas but in things,"[114] echoed by Snyder
in the poem "Riprap,"

all change, in thoughts,
As well as things,"

and who wrote his late poetry in bare American lines, as in
"Asphodel, That Greeny Flower" (1955):[63]

Starting to come down
by a new path
I at once found myself surrounded

by gypsy women
who came up to me,
I could speak little Spanish,
and directed me,
guided by a young girl,
on my way.
These were the pinnacles.

Nick Selby, writing about "Mid-August," reminds us, ". . .it is a work-poem. Work as a lookout depends upon visual experience, on the act of looking. The narrator is thus defined by his relationship to the landscape because of his work of reading it for signs of fire."[115] This gives an edge to the "smoke haze, three days heat, pitch glows": they aren't simply poetic descriptions, but possible bulletins. When he's looking down for miles, he isn't gazing, but doing his job. When asked what appealed to him in Chinese poetry, Snyder answered: "The secular quality, the engagement with history, the avoidance of theology or of elaborate symbolism or metaphor, the spirit of friendship, the openness to work, and, of course the sensibility for nature."[6] This work involves looking through the screen of nature to its underlying truth, as Selby shows: "The valley is seen through haze; 'rocks and meadows' are seen through swarms of flies; and, importantly, the poem's final image looks down at the environment surrounding Sourdough Mountain 'Through high still air.'" In a like way, ". . .we see the landscape through the poem. . ."[115]

The intensity of the watch dissolves him into the larger world, so that when he appears in the poem, it's only to say what he has forgotten and who he isn't seeing. The I disappears from the last lines, as after a sip of cold mountain water, there is only "Looking down for miles."

The book's title is taken from its last poem,[111] which begins

Lay down these words
Before your mind like rocks.
placed solid, by hands

The word "riprap" is explained in two lines of blank verse:

Riprap: a cobble of stone laid on steep slick rock
to make a trail for horses in the mountains

This sees words as stones, and poetry as work. This is connected with Snyder's view of what it is to be Beat: "That kind of choice really is what lies behind the Beat movement. . . As far as we were concerned, it was a choice of remaining laborers for the rest of our lives to be able to be poets."

At the 6 Gallery reading, reported by Kerouac in *The Dharma Bums*, Snyder read "A Berry Feast";[30] he has recorded various poems. On this experience, he said, "So poetry readings as a new cultural form enhanced and strengthened poetry itself, and the role of the poet. They also taught us that poetry really is an oral art."[113] In 1958, the Cold Mountain poems were first published in the *Evergreen Review*; in 1959, *Riprap* came out from Origin Press, with ten other equally compressed nature poems, and ten looser poems drawn from other sides of his life. In 1965, the Four Seasons Foundation, created in San Francisco by Don Allen, who edited the essential anthology *The New American Poetry: 1945-1960*, published *Riprap & Cold Mountain Poems* together,[105] another in the series of composite Beat poetry books.

Kerouac, in *The Dharma Bums*, into which variants of Cold Mountain Poems 3, 8, and 10, are woven, characterizes Snyder's poetry: ". . .he had his tender lyrical lines. . . and great mystery lines. . . his sudden bar-room humor. . . And his anarchistic ideas. . . His voice was deep and resonant and somehow brave, like the voice of oldtime American heroes and orators. Something earnest and strong and humanly hopeful. . ."[30] Glyn Maxwell sees his work stemming from *Riprap*: "The shapes and strengths of Gary Snyder's craft were established at the outset of his career. His first book, *Riprap*. . . , demonstrates the clarity of his seeing, his desire to crystallize moments, his striking ability to convey the physical nature of an instant. . ."[116] Gary Snyder's spirit turned to its magnetic north, China, and out of that contact,

he has created a new American voice, in work songs, balancing
with the natural, and fresh as air.

Philip Whalen drifted into the San Francisco renaissance, behind his old college roommate Gary Snyder:

> "Anyway, at some point I went back down again and wandered around, and then I came back up here and joined Gary who had found an apartment on Telegraph Hill he could share with me. And at that time, he had started going to Cal as a special student in Chinese and Japanese because he wanted to find what the Zen business was about from the inside, which took a lot of language. And so, anyhow, there were various moves and switches and whatnot, and in 1955 Ginsberg and Kerouac showed up, and we began. . . the revolution. . . [A]round 1959 LeRoi Jones wanted me to give him a book manuscript, so I sent him off the book that became *Like I Say*."[7]

Snyder's summer job as lookout at Sourdough Mountain in 1953 led to Whalen's stays there in the following two years, inspiring the long poem "Sourdough Mountain Lookout." "He began [it] there in the lookout on August 15, 1955. . . But he didn't really finish it until later on, after he met Allen Ginsberg. . . Philip was rooming with Ginsberg in Berkeley and watching over Ginsberg's shoulder as Allen was putting together the manuscript of 'Howl' for publication in 1956. I believe he was particularly impressed with Ginsberg's freedom of juxtaposition, and he saw how he could take a lot of the fragments that he had worked on in the lookout the year before and arrange them formally on the page."[118] Whalen said it showed him it was "possible for a poem to be its own shape and size."[4]

It was first published in the *Chicago Review* as an extract which included almost all of the last two pages. It appeared complete in *Like I Say*,[117] with the conclusion slightly revised, and then as an extract in *The New American Poetry: 1945–1960*,[2] again slightly revised. This is the complete text from that edition:

Beat Poetry

Excerpt: Sourdough Mountain Lookout

From Sauk Lookout two years before
Some of the view was down the Skagit
To Puget Sound: From above the lower ranges,
Deep in forest — lighthouses on clear nights.

This year's rock is a spur from the main range
Cuts the valley in two and is broken
By the river; Ross dam repairs the break,
Makes trolley buses run
Through the streets of dim Seattle far away.

I'm surrounded by mountains here
A circle of 108 beads, originally seeds
      of *ficus religiosa*
        BO-Tree
A circle, continuous, one odd bead
Larger than the rest and bearing
A tassel (hair-tuft) (the man who sat
      under the tree)
In the center of the circle,
A void, an empty figure containing
All that's multiplied;
Each bead a repetition, a world
Of ignorance and sleep.

Today is the day the goose gets cooked
Day of liberation for the crumbling flower
Knobcone pinecone in the flames
Brandy in the sun

Which, as I said, will disappear
Anyway it'll be invisible soon
Exchanging places with stars now in my head
To be growing rice in China through the night.
Magnetic storms across the solar plains

Make aurora borealis shimmy bright
Beyond the mountains to the north.

Closing the lookout in the morning
Thick ice on the shutters
Coyote almost whistling on a nearby ridge

The mountain is THERE (between two lakes)
I brought back a piece of its rock
Heavy dark-honey-color
With a seam of crystal, some of the quartz
Stained by its matrix
Practically indestructible
A shift from opacity to brilliance
(The zenbos say, "Lightning-flash & flint-spark")
Like the mountains where it was made

What we see of the world is the mind's
Invention and the mind
Though stained by it, becoming
Rivers, sun, mule-dung, flies —
Can shift instantly
A dirty bird in a square time

Gone	Gate
Gone	Gate
Really gone	Paragate
Into the cool.	Parasamgate
Oh Mama!	Svaha!

Like they say, "Four times up,
Three times down." I'm still on the mountain.

1955-56

This is a loose sutra, in the sense of oral scripture, beginning with direct observation, from lookouts past and present, moving through meditation on the mountains, and ending with observation of the mind, a mantra, and a proverb. In it, the poet's solitude leans naturally from experience of mountain, pinecone, sun, coyote, to musing on realities of mind.

Oriental references are noted: First, "A circle of 108 beads" is a mala, the Buddhist rosary, which the poet sees as mountain peaks. Second, "Lightning-flash & flint-spark" is the Buddhist saying, "Inadzuma no hikari, ishi no hi." It can refer to the brevity of existence, or sudden enlightenment. Third, "Gate gate / Paragate / Parasamgate / Bodhi svaha" is the mantra concluding the *Prajnaparamita Hridaya Sutra*, or the *Heart Sutra*, an early Buddhist text in Sanskrit and Chinese, said to be by Avalokitesvara, which Whalen translates into Beat slang with perfect accuracy. For example, Oh Mama! is sudden enlightenment: this sutra is one of the Perfection of Wisdom texts of Mahayana Buddhist literature, in which it's common to refer to the Perfection of Wisdom as the Mother of Buddhas. Fourth, "Four times up, three times down" is a deep variation on the proverb "Nana korobi, ya oki," "Seven times down, eight times up," meaning Perseverance furthers, first recorded in *Hagakure, Hidden by the Leaves*, 1716, a book on samurai by Yamamoto Tsunetomo: "People at the time of Lord Katsushige used to say, 'If one has not been a ronin at least seven times, he will not be a true retainer. Seven times down, eight times up.' . . .One should understand that it is something like being a self-righting doll."[119]

"Sourdough Mountain Lookout" is laid out as a free-verse ode, each irregular stanza arising from a focus, going from then to now, far to here, visible to invisible, rock to mind. Lines that would stretch too long are broken and indented. There are natural blank verse lines, "Magnetic storms across the solar plains," but line length varies freely. In, for example, the second stanza, almost every major category word plays a part in the music, with quiet alliteration, "rock / range / river / Ross / repairs, spur / streets / Seattle," and assonance, "rock / Ross / trolley, cuts /

buses / run, valley / trolley," and this sequence makes the stanza slant-rhyme abaca: "main / range / break / makes / away."

The diction is as free as line and stanza, ranging from counterculture slang, in "gone," defined previously, and "cool," to scientific idiom, "*ficus religiosa*, Magnetic storms, aurora borealis, crystal, quartz, matrix, opacity." Whalen follows Snyder in writing without metaphor or metonymy, except for the colloquial "dirty bird."

As with Gary Snyder, William Carlos Williams' visit to Reed College was crucial, as indicated in this interchange:

> "Philip Whalen: Well the thing that was important to me at that particular time was the *Paterson* material that was coming out. . . I think that *Paterson Three* had come out by the time he was up there. And so it was very exciting to talk to him about some of it. . .
> David Meltzer: I can see *Paterson* in relationship to lots of your work with those kinds of streams and strands of heard language and written language and also this notion of the concreteness as the source of this mystery.
> Philip Whalen: 'No ideas but in things.'"[7]

This passage from *Paterson*, Book II: "Sunday in the Park",[120] underlies "Sourdough Mountain Lookout:"

> Without invention nothing is well spaced,
> unless the mind change, unless
> the stars are new measured, according
> to their relative positions, the
> line will not change, the necessity
> will not matriculate: unless there is
> a new mind there cannot be a new
> line, the old will go on
> repeating itself with recurring
> deadliness: without invention
> nothing lies under the witch-hazel
> bush, the alder does not grow from among

the hummocks margining the all
but spent channels of the old swale,
the small foot-prints
of mice under the overhanging
tufts of the bunch-grass will not
appear: without invention the line
will never again take on its ancient
divisions when the word, a supple word,
lived in it, crumbled now to chalk.

Both passages are meditations—one in a park, the other in mountains—on the mind's invention, and share those words, as well as "stars, tuft, repeating / repetition, change / exchanging."

Whalen's sutra follows thought naturally: this lookout puts him in mind of last year's and its view; he returns to this year's, whose circle of mountains reminds him of a loop of beads, seeds of the tree under which Gautama Buddha was enlightened; he thinks of what he'll eat and drink, of the sun and its passing, to shine on China all night; he notes local ice, hears coyote, considers the rock he brought back from a ridge, and its light; then he sees all sensation as the mind's invention, as it becomes what it beholds. This enlightenment sparks the mantra, "gone," and the poem ends on a proverb which says that the poet is beat / beatific: though he's back in the city, writing, his spirit's still in the mountain wilderness.

Ginsberg loved to quote Whalen: "My writing is a picture of the mind moving."[121] "He can make anything work. . ."[124] says Lew Welch. *Like I Say*,[117] published by Totem/Corinth in 1960, opens with "Plus Ça Change. . .," which Whalen recited at the 6 Gallery reading, has twenty-five poems, including sprawling texts cobbled from notebooks, intense lyrics, a superb blank verse ode, "For C.," and concludes with the complete "Sourdough Mountain Lookout." He has been filmed and recorded reading poetry.[83] Tom Devaney says, "In Whalen, the poetry is a continuous interplay of prose, verse, historical fragments and native speech shaping and genre-shifting their idiomatic presence towards the real."[122]

Lew Welch, like Ginsberg, was drawn out of advertising into poetry. Following his college roommates Snyder and Whalen, he had himself transferred by a department store from Chicago to San Francisco, where he quit, drove a cab, and joined the renaissance.

Welch tells how "Ring of Bone"[123] came to be written: there was a breakup followed by isolation in the wilderness, and a vision:

"She is weeping at the top of the stairs, and I am weeping at the bottom of the stairs, and like there are no words left. And we are both poets. And she knows I've got to leave, yet she really doesn't know why.

Ferlinghetti loaned me his cabin in Big Sur. I went to him and said: 'Look, man, it's really freak-city time. Can I borrow your cabin?'

He's beautiful that way. Sure. And bang, here's the key. OK, so down I go. I take enough groceries to last about two weeks and a typewriter and a lot of paper, and I just thrashed around in it. And one day, I got it.

I woke up after a wine drunk—I had brought a lot of red wine with me—I woke up about three in the afternoon and I saw it."[7]

I saw myself
a ring of bone
in the clear stream
of all of it

and vowed
always to be open to it
that all of it
might flow through

and then heard
"ring of bone" where
ring is what a

bell does

This lyric is intensified by its extremity: its twelve lines are mostly four syllables or less. Each word is more naked, more fraught. It's a single sentence, as if spoken, and so, paratactic: "I saw... and vowed... and then heard." It's remarkable for its lack of allusion to anything outside its vision. It's in three quatrains, with the last line separated, for a rest, before the concluding music. In these close quarters, there is a triple chime of "ring," "all / always / all," and "it"; "bone" resounds against "open" and "flow," and then against "bell." The words used are as simple as possible.

The figure, "ring of bone," is, as the poem says, used doubly, as an emptiness that reality flows through, and as the resonance of a struck bell. "Bone" takes him to the root of himself, his structure and destiny, skeleton. "Ring" redeems all: as opening to life, as music in answer.

As with Snyder and Whalen, William Carlos Williams' visit and reading at their college was vital. "We took him to our pad, where Whalen and Snyder and I lived, and we played poetry games and talked, and we gave him our stuff... It was pure mind transmission."[7] The game was "improvising poems around five randomly chosen words."[4] Welch derived poetry as direct, simple, spoken, in lines of few syllables, from him, as in his late flowering, "Asphodel, That Greeny Flower":[63]

> I have forgot
>> and yet I see clearly enough
>>> something
>
> central to the sky
>> which ranges round it.
>>> An odor
>
> springs from it!
>> A sweetest odor!
>>> Honeysuckle!

"Ring of Bone" is from *Hermit Poems*;[123] it and its companion volume, *The Way Back*,[125] sound like a T'ang dynasty poet brought back. In a major essay, "Language Is Speech," speaking of the poet as visionary, he said:

> "He is in a trance. And all he is trying to do is make his living writing baby-talk ads for a mail-order house.
>
> But Li Po, while extemporizing intricate lines on whatever subject the Emperor happened to throw at him, dropped, I am sure, into the same glazed-eyed state. His eyes would then clear, and he'd wittily speak his lines.
>
> I saw William Carlos Williams do this on a challenge from Snyder and Whalen and me in 1950."[124]

Welch may be referring to a specific occasion where Li Po was called for by the emperor; it also involves a woman, and wine:

> "One day in spring Hsuan Tsung with Lady Yang Kuei-fei held a royal feast in the Pavilion of Aloes. The tree-peonies of the garden, newly imported from India, were in full flower as if in rivalry of beauty with the emperor's voluptuous mistress. There were the musicians of the Pear Garden and the wine of grapes from Hsi-liang. Li Po was summoned, for only his art could capture for eternity the glory of the vanishing hours. But when brought to the imperial presence, the poet was drunk. Court attendants threw cold water on his face and handed him a writing brush. Whereupon he improvised those three beautiful songs in rapturous praise of Yang Kuei-fei, while the emperor himself played the tune on a flute of jade."

A Song of Pure Happiness
(Written to Music for Lady Yang)

I

Her robe is a cloud, her face a flower;
Her balcony, glimmering with the bright spring dew,
Is either the tip of earth's Jade Mountain
Or a moon-edged roof of Paradise.

II

There's a perfume stealing moist from a shaft of red
      blossom,
And a mist, through the heart, from the magical Hill of
      Wu—
The palaces of China have never known such beauty—
Not even Flying Swallow with all her glittering
      garments.

III

Lovely now together, his lady and his flowers
Lighten forever the Emperor's eye,
As he listens to the sighing of the far spring wind
Where she leans on a railing in the Aloe Pavilion.[127]

Between the two poets, the occasion is the same after-wine musing and sensual provocation, and the poems have the same tendency to slip into the mystic, whether ring of bone and the clear stream, or roof of Paradise and magical Hill.

Welch said:

"There is something that is not us, right? Now for me, it is this earth that I stand on, these trees, this sweet air, the lovely water I drink, the fish that swim in it. . . all of this is a source of endless wonder. But it is the see-er in us who, as Stein put it, can 'know themselves knowing it.' We are the poets. . . Because it is right there under your feet, see? And it is not only your feet and your eyes that let you 'know yourself knowing it.' It's God.

Those are visions. They are things that you can see. You can see them. They are not special states of mind, although when I see them at times, the ecstasies get to the point that it is physically painful. I actually writhe like I am in a fit and I weep and I bellow. And that is the source of my poems."[7]

He revisits this inspiration in the beginning of a poem written as preface to his collected poems, *Ring of Bone*:[126]

To the memory of

Gertrude Stein & William Carlos Williams

I WANT THE WHOLE THING, the moment
when what we thought was rock, or
sea
became clear Mind, and

what we thought was clearest Mind really
was that glancing girl, that
swirl of birds . . .

(all of that)

He is immersed in the waters of experience, "in the clear stream / of all of it. . . that all of it / might flow through."[123] The poet as subject and the world as object vanish; there is only the opening in the bone through which the stream flows, and the bone as a bell ringing out poetry. Though beat after a wine drunk, he is open to the beatific, embodying Kerouac's definition of this counterculture.

Seven of the ten *Hermit Poems*, including "[I saw myself]", were recorded at the Mad Monster Mammoth Poets' Reading in 1963,[83] radiant with humor. The book,[123] in his own calligraphy, was published by the Four Seasons Foundation in 1965. *The Way Back*, with twelve poems, including three in prose, was unpublished till *Selected Poems*,[125] where the two books, connected but variant, as with other Beat poetry texts, appear together complete.

In his biography, Aram Saroyan says, "The further afield he went in terms of the society of his time, the more remarkable and authentic was the poetry that came out of his life."[128] Snyder says, "The heart of the book is the 'Hermit Poems' and 'Way Back' sections—poems evoking, covering, the time spent in retreat and practice at a cabin in the mountains of coast north California deep up rivers, still Yurok land. In those works, Lew really achieved the meeting of an ancient sage-tradition, the 'shack simple' post-frontier back country out-of-work workingman's style, and the rebel modernism of art."[125] Like his college roommates, Snyder and Whalen, Lew Welch went beyond study of the Orient to living it out, in the tradition of Taoist and Zen hermit poets. After the wine wears off, there is a vision.

7th Chorus:
Jazz:
David Meltzer /
Bob Kaufman

David Meltzer was writing poetry in Hollywood, when he followed the artist, poet, and publisher Wallace Berman to San Francisco:

> "He came for the weekend, and I came because I had a job working at a place called Paper Editions, a job I got through Norman Rose, who owned the bookstore where I first saw the Bermans. I don't know what year it was, but the first Pocket Poets books had come out. I remember reading Ferlinghetti at the open-air newsstand on Highland Avenue and Hollywood Boulevard. I thought, this is great, little books of poems. I remember that when *Howl* came out, that was a great opening up and out. . ."[7]

Berman went on to publish Meltzer's *The Clown*, as well as the broadside of McClure's *Peyote Poem*.

In the new city, Meltzer wrote a series of 25 Ragas:[129]

6th RAGA / for Bob Alexander

The cigarette gone, you walked
over to the stain where
the sea last hit the shore
&, with your fingers, began
drawing the outline of a woman
into the sand. Her body —
her breasts: a poke
inside each center for
her nipples. Her cunt —
a simple v, & her hair,
a spray of seaweed found nearby,
some twigs.

Jumping back, the sea rushing in,
you yelled out something very loud —
but the ocean was louder.
I didn't hear.
We turned our back on the Pacific,
the mural of your woman,
letting them do battle unseen.
Back up to Ocean Front Avenue.
Charlie was waiting with his camera,
Altoon had arrived with a 6-pack
of good old Lucky Lager Beer.

This is an anecdote, in natural language: four friends hanging out in Venice, California: David Meltzer, poet, Bob Alexander, artist, Charles Brittin, photographer, and John Altoon, painter. All appeared in Wallace Berman's underground art and poetry magazine, *Semina*. It has the air of a snapshot, though the language has undercurrents. In his *New American Poetry* biographical note, Meltzer says, "At 14 I left for the West & stayed in L. A., for 6 formative years in which I met Wallace Berman & Robert Alexander, who were instrumental in turning me on to the fantastic possibilities of art & the self."[2] In this light, "6th Raga" can be seen as a spiritual lesson on transience and creation.

Raga is a classical Indian music form, improvisation within constraints. Meltzer talks of his encounter: "My first night in San Francisco at Lee & Idell Romero's Potrero pad — had flown up from L.A. w/ Wallace Berman — heard an Angel LP of Ragas by Ravi Shankar w/ Yehudi Menuhin giving a small talk on the modes & scales & I said this sounds like jazz to me, this sounds like poetic practice."[132] This refers to the first appearance of classical Indian music in the West, on the albums "Music of India, Volume 1 and 2," from 1955 and 1956, with ragas played by Ali Akbar Khan on the first—Rag Sindhu Bhairavi and Rag Pilu Baroowa; and Ravi Shankar on the second—Raga Ahir Bhairav, Raga Simhendra Madhyamam, and Raga Jog. Ten years later, raga music was embraced by the West, but to call a series of poems Ragas in the mid-fifties was prescient. "Raga" is Sanskrit for "what colors the mind."

The procedure in raga, improvising around a scale rather than a melody, was being explored intuitively in the late fifties by the jazz master Miles Davis, resulting in the consummate "Kind of Blue." At the same time, Meltzer was reciting poetry to jazz at a San Francisco club: "Started reading at The Cellar in '58 when I was 21. Jim Dickson up from L.A. & caught my set & flew me down South for a gig at the Renaissance Club on Sunset & after hours recorded an album which finally came out a few months ago."[132] Bill Morgan says, "He arrived with only the outline of a poem and improvised the wording and cadence in sync with the music."[10] Karl Young talks about how this works: "One of David Meltzer's practices in verse composition is to start with a simple, basic, elemental idea and build on it, taking in associations and improvisations as he goes. It is a method almost identical to that of the classic jazz musicians he admires and from whom he has learned. . ."[133] McClure adds, "David was a musician, so he had an advantage. . . Meltzer could compose his poems for poetry and jazz with the idea that he was another instrument in a combo."[21] Meltzer finishes: "Then it's like playing jazz — you have like a head arrangement and everyone knows pretty much where the song is going, but in the interim, when you start improvising and dialoguing, it takes turns. . ."[134] The album was released nearly a half century later as "Poet w / Jazz 1958".[130]

"6th Raga" is divided into two essentially equal stanzas, which balance each other substantively, and though lines vary from two to ten syllables, they average seven syllables, and half of them are seven or eight syllables, suggesting that there is a paradigm of eight syllables, as in "a spray of seaweed found nearby," and other lines are variants. The two main images, sea and body, are conveyed in two series of words connected by alliteration on their opening consonants: "cigarette, stain, sea, sand, center, simple, spray, seaweed, sea, unseen, 6-pack / body, breasts, nearby, back, but, back, battle, Beer."

The poem is David recalling another time together, for Bob. The diction is colloquial, as in a conversation among bohemians, so that even "cunt" is natural. The drawing of a woman in the sand and the oncoming tide take on symbolic values as art and time. This is elaborated: not only is the artist's mural washed over by the waves, but his yell is overcome by their breaking.

Meltzer mentions diverse early influences: Emily Dickinson, Carl Sandburg, T. S. Eliot, E. E. Cummings, William Carlos Williams, Ogden Nash, Dylan Thomas, Paul Éluard, Louis Aragon, Jules Supervielle, and the experimental prose of James Joyce, John Dos Passos, and Kenneth Patchen: "Robert Duncan said, poets are like magpies: they grab at anything bright, and they take it back to their nest, and they'll use it sooner or later. I used everything, everything that shone for me." "6th Raga"

Larry Beckett

can be read as an improvisation on an Italian sonnet, with its first half statement, turn, and second half counterstatement. This method, with classic structure and experimental layout, is seen in E. E. Cummings' *Tulips & Chimneys*, "Sonnets—Unrealities" (1923):[135]

XVI

when citied day with the sonorous homes
of light swiftly sink in the sorrowful hour,
they counted petals O tremendous flower
on whose huge heart prospecting darkness roams

torture my spirit with the exquisite froms
and whithers of existence,
                 as by shores
soundless, the unspeaking watcher who adores

perceived sails whose mighty brightness dumbs

the utterance of his soul—so even I
wholly chained to a grave astonishment
feel in my being the delirious smart

of thrilled ecstasy, where sea and sky
marry—

       to know the white ship of my heart

    on frailer ports of costlier commerce bent

With lines broken and separated by space, this doesn't look like an Italian sonnet. But it's in fourteen lines of iambic pentameter, with slant rhymes. The structure of that form is: statement, turn away, counterstatement. That armature is only slightly submerged in this seaside poem: any "unspeaking watcher", "so even I", personal "ecstasy."

129

"6th Raga" approximates a blank verse sonnet, again with a variable layout. It opens and closes with pleasures, the end of a smoke for the artist, and the beginning of liquor for the companions. The artist creates an assemblage of a nude, out of finger drawing, seaweed, twigs—whatever's at hand. This is done right where "the sea last hit the shore," a guarantee the waves will erase it, setting up time against art. Nature and time are immediately reasserted, as the sea rushes in, drowning out the artist's voice as well. But then something new occurs: after raising these deep intellectual antinomies, the poet drops them, and the sonnet's turn is literal: "We turned our back on the Pacific," art is abandoned to the waves, as the boys go for a beer. This is an American gesture, especially of the far West, aware, anti-intellectual. The artist creates, and then relaxes; time takes care of eternity. There's no need to meditate these complexities; it'd be better just to hang out on Ocean Front Avenue. With a drawing in sand, bottles on the street, they're beatific and beat down, as Kerouac worked out the definition of beat.[34]

Ragas, from 1959, is not only another composite Beat text, but is remarkable as a book conceived as lyrics combined with a set of extracts from longer works: a journal; "25 Ragas"; "The Hollywood Poem"; "Night Before Morning"; "The Clown"; "Ward Poems."

Meltzer has achieved in lyric, narrative, song, essay, interview, anthology, erotic novel. In the foreword to his selected poems, Michael Rothenberg says, "When I read David's poetry, read his words, I think of alchemical conjuring, zen, beat, jazz rhythms, prayer, the everyday in a moment-flash, historical overviews, urban and domestic reflections."[131] Dale Smith speaks of his "improvisational charm and gnostic vision. Care for language is not to make it obscure but to use it as a tool for discovery."[136] *Ragas* was published by Discovery Books "when I worked at The Discovery Bookshop on Columbus, a few doors below City Lights."[132] David Meltzer explores the border between composition and improvisation, whole and fragment, word as meaning and as melody. Orality and musicality, with which Homer opened this art, too often lost, live in his gigs and lines.

We meet Bob Kaufman in the actual street. Because of his recitations and impromptus in San Francisco jazz clubs, coffee houses, bars, restaurants, and traffic jams, he was known as The Original Be-Bop Man. Poetry like jazz belongs not on the page but in the air, spontaneous, in a voice. He had moved from New York to San Francisco in the company of Ginsberg, and became a comrade of Meltzer. With Ginsberg, Ferlinghetti, and others, he edited the magazine *Beatitude*: a "weekly miscellany of poetry and other jazz designed to extol beauty and promote the beatific life among the various mendicants, neo-existentialists, christs, poets, painters, musicians, and other inhabitants and observers of North Beach, San Francisco, California, United States of America."[141] The name "Beatitude" derives from Jack Kerouac's definition of beat as beat down and beatific;[34] he is the incarnation. He is Ginsberg's "bum and angel beat."[55]

He was a friend of the bop jazz saxophonist Charlie Parker, "a poet in jazz," and it's said that at Kerouac's suggestion he named his son Parker. This sets up a double reference in this lyric:[139]

Walking Parker Home

Sweet beats of jazz impaled on slivers of wind
Kansas Black Morning/ First Horn Eyes/
Historical sound pictures on New Bird wings
People shouts/ boy alto dreams/ Tomorrow's
Gold belled pipe of stops and future Blues Times
Lurking Hawkins/ shadows of Lester/ realization
Bronze fingers—brain extensions seeking trapped
       sounds
Ghetto thoughts/ bandstand courage/ solo flight
Nerve-wracked suspicions of newer songs and doubts
New York altar city/ black tears/ secret disciples
Hammer horn pounding soul marks on unswinging
       gates
Culture gods/ mob sounds/ visions of spikes
Panic excursions to tribal Jazz wombs and transfusions
Heroin nights of birth/ and soaring/ over boppy new
       ground
Smothered rage covering pyramids of notes
       spontaneously exploding
Cool revelations/ shrill hopes/ beauty speared into
       greedy ears
Birdland nights on bop mountains, windy saxophone
       revolutions
Dayrooms of junk/ and melting walls and circling
       vultures/
Money cancer/ remembered pain/ terror flights/
Death and indestructible existence

In that Jazz corner of life
Wrapped in a mist of sound
His legacy, our Jazz-tinted dawn
Wailing his triumphs of oddly begotten dreams
Inviting the nerveless to feel once more
That fierce dying of humans consumed
In raging fires of Love.

Larry Beckett

This is a series of impressions which portray Charlie Parker; it's open-eyed to his pain in life, his art in beauty. He was born in Kansas; his predecessors at the jazz saxophone include Coleman Hawkins and Lester Young; at 19 he moved to New York City; he was nicknamed Yardbird, then Bird, and the nightclub Birdland was named after him; bebop, bop, is the music he invented. The poem is structured in two parts; a portrait, in a set of appositives, qualified nouns evoking Bird's life and art: "beats, jazz, slivers, wind, Morning, Eyes, pictures, wings, shouts, dreams, pipe, stops, Times, shadows, fingers, extensions, sounds, thoughts, courage, flight. . . " and a brief coda on his legacy.

The line in the first long stanza is loose blank verse, starting on a stress, a downbeat: "Sweet, Kansas, People, Gold, Lurking, Bronze, Ghetto, Nerve. . ." This stress works differently from line to line: in the first, it replaces a slack; in the second, slack and stress are reversed; in the twelfth, the opening slack is dropped, leaving the stress. The second stanza makes its own music, with briefer lines. The line can be long in this lyric, and so it's articulated by slashes, which make it waver, in phrases, like the lines of Bird. The poem begins with internal rhymes: "sweet beats, Morning / Horn"; and continues by alliterations derived from the first sound in "Bird: Black / Bird / boy / belled / blues / Bronze / brain / bandstand / black / birth / boppy / beauty / Birdland / bop." Musician's slang comes naturally, in "bop" for jazz and "junk" for heroin.

The first line introduces the main figure, balancing music and pain: "Sweet beats of jazz impaled on slivers of wind," where the wind is Bird's breath through the horn, and the way of the world. The pain of prejudice shows in "trapped, Ghetto, suspicions, doubts, spikes, Panic, rage, vultures, cancer, pain, terror, Death"; the answer in music shows in "jazz, Horn, alto, belled, pipe, Blues, sounds, bandstand, solo, songs, notes, ears."

Kaufmann is connected to the Spanish surrealist poet and dramatist Federico Garcia Lorca, and references him continually, as in the poem "Lorca":[140]

Spit olive pits at my Lorca,
Give Harlem's king one spoon,
At four in the never moon.
Scoop out the croaker eyes
    of rose flavored Gypsies
Singing Garcia,
In lost Spain's
Darkened noon.

Neeli Cherkovski elaborates on this: "Lorca saw great poetry, and all great art, as possessed of *duende*, a mysterious essence that radiates from within, having little to do with a preconceived idea of craft and more with an embodied spirit that somehow captures the purest essence of what it means to be human. . . Kaufman longed to embrace this spirit of *duende*. . . [and] strove for the clarity of expression and the intensity found in Lorca's poems. . ."[88] "Gypsies" alludes to Lorca's classic *Gypsy Ballads* (1928), "four in the never moon" to "five in the afternoon" in the *Lament for Ignacio Sanchez Mejias* (1935), and "Harlem's king" to that poem in *Poet in New York* (1930), which inspired a phrase in Ginsberg's "Howl," and whose poem for another iconic American artist, "Ode to Walt Whitman",[142] gives the scene and structure of "Walking Parker Home:"

from
Ode to Walt Whitman

New York of muck,
New York of mire and of death.
What angel is hidden in your cheek?
What perfect voice will speak the truth of the wheat?
Who, that terrible dream of your stained wildflowers?

Not for one single moment, beautiful old Walt
    Whitman,
have I ever ceased seeing your beard full of butterflies,
or your corduroy shoulders worn thin by the moonlight,

or your thighs of a virginal Apollo,
or your voice just like a column of ash;
aged one, as beautiful as the mists,
who wailed the same as a bird
with its sex pierced by a needle.
Enemy of the satyr,
Enemy of the vine,
and lover of bodies beneath coarse cloth.

This poem recalls Ginsberg's "Howl," with "mire" and "angel," and lines beginning "who." Like "Walking Parker Home," it's set in New York, arcs from death to love, and is dedicated to a major American artist, portrayed as a series of qualified nouns, and oscillates between dream images of pain and creation: "muck, mire, death, terrible, stained, worn, thin, ash, wailed, pierced, needle, Enemy, coarse / angel, voice, speak, truth, wheat, dream, wildflowers, beautiful, butterflies, thighs, Apollo, voice, beautiful, bird, sex, vine, lover: who wailed the same as a bird."

"Walking Parker Home" is the poet walking his son home, and meditating on the artist he named him after. "Take it home" is what jazz musicians say when they're going into the last chorus. After a line mirroring the beauty and pain of Bird's blues, the poem goes through his birth, boyhood, predecessors, fulfillment, fears, drugs, and into his revolutionary music. In the end, though jazz is only part of life, it can color the morning, give hope of victory, and waken dead nerve endings to the ultimate in pain and music, mortality in love. In "War Memoir: Jazz, Don't Listen To At Your Own Risk",[140] he says explicitly how he balances, against suffering, the redemption of jazz:

> jazz, scratching, digging, bluing, swinging jazz,
> And we listen
> And we feel
> And live

His prose poetry *Abomunist Manifesto*[137] and *Second*

April[138] were published by Ferlinghetti's City Lights. His first book, *Solitudes Crowded with Loneliness*,[139] was assembled by others, from transcriptions, tapes, scraps of paper, notebooks, manuscripts, and published by New Directions.

One of his editors says of his art, "Adapting the harmonic complexities and spontaneous invention of be-bop to poetic euphony and meter, he became the quintessential jazz poet."[140] This is the music of an oral poetry, where composition happens in performance. A critic continues, "Embracing this bardic tradition of orality, the Beats borrowed from jazz the qualities of improvisation, muscular musicality, and direct transmission."[143] Speaking of Kaufman's recitations from others and inventions of his own, Natale Peditto says, "Poetry, for Kaufman, was always a part of the occasion for his utterances and inseparable from the activities of his daily life. . . Rather than a distanced, abstract poetry of the formal, printed 'literary' type, this Beat poet was aware of and engaged his audience's immediate senses in a poetry of the body."[144] Bob Kaufman added beat as rhythm. He fused the tradition and the street in that San Francisco flowering, Beat poetry.

Reprise

Intro

1 Evergreen Review: Number 2. The San Francisco Scene. Edited by Donald Allen. New York: Grove Press, 1957.

2 The New American Poetry: 1945-1960. Edited by Donald Allen. New York: Grove Press, 1960; Berkeley: University of California Press, 1999.

3 The Portable Beat Reader. Edited by Ann Charters. New York: Viking, 1992.

4 The Birth of the Beat Generation. Steven Watson. New York: Pantheon Books, 1995.

5 The Beats: A Literary Reference. Edited by Matt Theado. New York: Carrol & Graf, 2003.

6 Beat Writers at Work. Edited by George Plimpton. New York: Modern Library, 1999.

7 San Francisco Beat: Talking with the Poets. Edited by David Meltzer. San Francisco: City Lights Books, 2001.

8 The Beat Vision: A Primary Sourcebook. Edited by Arthur Knight and Kit Knight. New York: Paragon House Publishers, 1987.

9 Beat Generation: Glory Days in Greenwich Village.

Fred McDarrah. New York: Schirmer Books, 1996.

10   The Beat Generation in San Francisco: A Literary
     Tour. Bill Morgan. San Francisco: City Lights Books,
     2003.

11   Princeton Encyclopedia of Poetry and Poetics
     (Enlarged Edition). Edited by Alex Preminger. New
     Jersey: Princeton University Press, 1974.

Lawrence Ferlinghetti

12   Pictures of the gone world. San Francisco: City Lights
     Books, 1955. Reissued in 1995 with "18 new verses."

13   Pictures of the Gone World. Synergy cd, 2005. With
     David Amram.

14   Poetry Readings in the Cellar. Fantasy cd, 1957 /
     2004. With Cellar Jazz Quintet.

15   A Coney Island of the Mind. New York: New
     Directions Books, 1958.

16   A Coney Island of the Mind. With Dana Colley.
     Rykodisc cd, 1999.

17   "Notes on Poetry in San Francisco." A Casebook on
     the Beat. Edited by Thomas Parkinson. New York:
     Thomas Y. Crowell, 1961.

18   "San Francisco Poet Laureate Inaugural Address."
     San Francisco: Poetry Flash, 1998.

19   Finnegans Wake. James Joyce. London: Faber &
     Faber, 1939.

20   "A Throw of the Dice." Collected Poems. Stéphane
     Mallarmé, translated by Henry Weinfeld. Berkeley:
     University of California Press, 1994.

21   Ferlinghetti: the Artist in His Time. Barry Silesky.
     New York: Warner Books, 1990.

22   "The Swan." Imitations. Charles Baudelaire,translated
     by Robert Lowell. New York: Farrar, Straus and
     Giroux, 1961.

23   Ferlinghetti: A Biography. Neeli Cherkovski. New
     York: Doubleday & Company, 1979.

24   "And the Fête Continues." Paroles. Jacques Prévert,

translated by Lawrence Ferlinghetti. San Francisco: City Lights Books, 1958.

25 The White Goddess. Robert Graves. New York: Farrar, Straus and Giroux: 1948, 1966.

26 "Naked and the Clad," M.L. Rosenthal. The Nation, 187 (October 11, 1958), 215.

Jack Kerouac

27 On the Road. Written 1951-1952. New York: The Viking Press, 1957.

28 Visions of Cody. Written 1951-1952. New York: McGraw-Hill Book Company, 1974.

29 "The Railroad Earth." Written 1952. New York: McGraw-Hill Book Company, 1960.

30 The Dharma Bums. Written 1957. New York: The Viking Press, 1958.

31 Book of Blues. Written 1954-1961. New York: Penguin Books, 1995.

32 Mexico City Blues. Written 1955. New York: Grove Press, 1959.

33 Selected Letters: Volume 1. Written 1940-1956. Edited by Ann Charters New York: The Viking Press, 1995.

34 "About the Beat Generation." The Portable Jack Kerouac. Jack Kerouac, edited by Ann Charters. New York: Viking, 1957 / 1995.

35 Poetry for the Beat Generation. New York: Hanover, 1959 / The Jack Kerouac Collection. Rhino Records cd, Disc 1, 1990.

36 Blues and Haikus. New York: Hanover, 1959 / The Jack Kerouac Collection. Rhino Records cd, Disc 2, 1990.

37 Readings by Jack Kerouac on the Beat Generation. New York: Verve, 1960 / The Jack Kerouac Collection. Rhino Records cd, Disc 3, 1990.

38 Book of Haikus. Written 1956-1961. Edited by Regina Weinreich. New York: Penguin Books, 2003.

39 Lonesome Traveler. Written 1953-1960. New York: McGraw-Hill Book Company, 1960.

40 Desolation Angels. Written 1956, 1961. Coward-McCann, 1965.

41 Big Sur. Written 1961. Jack Kerouac. New York: Farrar, Straus and Cudahy, 1962.

42 Pull My Daisy. New York: Grove Press, 1961.

43 Scattered Poems. Written 1954-1965. Edited by Lawrence Ferlinghetti. San Francisco: City Lights Books, 1971.

44 Pomes All Sizes. Written 1945-1966. San Francisco: City Lights Books, 1992.

45 Selected Letters: Volume 2. Written 1957-1969. Edited by Ann Charters. New York: The Viking Press, 1999.

46 Kerouac's Spontaneous Poetic: A Study of the Fiction Regina Weinreich. New York: Thunder's Mouth Press, second edition, 2001.

47 Jack Kerouac. Tom Clark. New York: Harcourt Brace Jovanovich, 1984.

48 Hamlet. William Shakespeare. 1600.

49 Zen in English Literature and Oriental Classics. R. H. Blyth. Tokyo: The Hokuseido Press, 1942.

50 Haiku. Volumes 1 - 4. R. H. Blyth. Tokyo: The Hokuseido Press, 1947-1952.

51 The Way of Life According to Laotzu. Witter Bynner. New York: Farrar, Straus and Giroux, 1944, 1978.

52 Jack's Book: An Oral Biography of Jack Kerouac. Edited by Barry Gifford and Lawrence Lee. New York: St. Martin's Press, 1978.

Allen Ginsberg

53 Reality Sandwiches. Written 1953-1960. San Francisco: City Lights Books, 1963.

54 Howl: Original Draft Facsimile. New York: HarperCollins, 1988.

55 Howl and Other Poems. San Francisco: City Lights

Books, 1956.

56 On the Poetry of Allen Ginsberg. Edited by Lewis
    Hyde. Ann Arbor: University of Michigan Press,
    1984.

57 Collected Poems: 1947 – 1980. New York: Harper &
    Row, 1980.

58 Howl and Other Poems. Fantasy Records, 1959 /
    Howls, Raps Roars, Disc 2. Rhino Records cd, 1993.

59 Holy Soul Jelly Roll. Disc 1. Los Angeles: Rhino
    Records cd, 1994.

60 Leaves of Grass. Walt Whitman. New York: self-
    published, 1860.

61 "Psalm 103." David; Isaiah. King James Old
    Testament, 10th-1st centuries BCE.

62 The Bridge. Hart Crane. New York: Horace Liveright,
    1930.

63 Journey to Love. W. C. Williams. New York: Random
    House, 1955.

64 Scratching the Beat Surface. Michael McClure.
    Boulder: North Point Press, 1982.

65 The New Poets. M.L. Rosenthal. New York: Oxford
    University Press, 1967.

Gregory Corso

66 The Vestal Lady on Brattle and Other Poems.
    Cambridge: Richard Brukenfeld, 1955.

67 Gasoline. San Francisco: City Lights Books, 1958.

68 Bomb. San Francisco: City Lights Books, 1958.

69 The Happy Birthday of Death. New York: New
    Directions, 1960.

70 "Standing on a Street Corner: A Little Play." The
    Evergreen Review Reader: 1957-1966. A Ten-Year
    Anthology. Edited by Barney Rosset. New York:
    Castle, 1967.

71 "Interview with Michael Andre." Unmuzzled Ox 6.2,
    #22, Winter 1981.

72 An Accidental Autobiography: The Selected Letters.

Edited by Bill Morgan. New York: New Directions, 2003.

73   Die On Me. Koch Records cd, 2002.

74   Calligrammes: Poems of Peace and War, 1913-1916. Guillaume Apollinaire, translated by Anne Greet. Berkeley: University of California Press, 1991.

75   "The Altar." The Temple. George Herbert, 1633.

76   "Zone." Guillaume Apollinaire, translated by Dudley Fitts. An Anthology of French Poetry from Nerval to Valéry in English Translation with French Originals. Edited by Angel Flores. New York: Anchor Books, 1958.

77   "Ode to the West Wind." Prometheus Unbound. Percy Shelley, 1820.

78   "Somewhere Else with Allen and Gregory." Dom Moraes. Horizon 11.1, Winter 1969, 66-67.

79   Exiled Angel: A Study of the Work of Gregory Corso. Gregory Stephenson. London: Hearing Eye, 1989.

John Wieners

80   The Hotel Wentley Poems. San Francisco. Auerhahn Press, 1958.

81   The Hotel Wentley Poems: Original Versions. San Francisco: D. Haselwood, 1965.

82   Selected Poems, 1958 - 1984. Santa Barbara: Black Sparrow Press, 1986.

83   Howls, Raps & Roars. Disc 4. Rhino Records cd, 1993.

84   The journal of John Wieners is to be called 707 Scott Street for Billie Holiday, 1959. Los Angeles: Sun & Moon Press, 1996.

85   "Structure and Style in the Greater Romantic Lyric." M. H. Abrams. From Sensibility to Romanticism: Essays Presented to Frederick A. Pottle. Edited by Frederick W. Hilles and Harold Bloom, London: Oxford University Press, 1965.

86   "Work Without Hope." Poetical Works. S. T.

Coleridge, 1828.

87 "Les Luths." Second Avenue. Frank O'Hara. New York: Totem/Corinth, 1960.

88 Whitman's Wild Children: Portraits of Twelve Poets. Neeli Cherkovski. San Francisco: The Lapis Press, 1988.

89 Robert Creeley. The Hipster of Joy Street: An introduction to the life and work of John Wieners. Pamela Petro. Boston College Magazine, Fall 2000.

Michael McClure

90 Hymns to St. Geryon & Other Poems. San Francisco: Auerhahn Press, 1959.

91 Dark Brown. San Francisco: Auerhahn Press, 1961.

92 Hymns to St. Geryon & Dark Brown. London: Cape Goliard, 1969.

93 Hymns to St. Geryon & Dark Brown. Bolinas: Grey Fox Press, 1980.

94 Composed on the Tongue. Allen Ginsberg. Bolinas: Grey Fox Press, 1980.

95 Visions of the Daughters of Albion. William Blake, 1793.

96 Inferno. Dante Alighieri, translated by Henry Longfellow. Boston: Ticknor & Fields, 1867.

97 The Daybreak Boys: Essays on the Literature of the Beat Generation. Gregory Stephenson. Carbondale: Southern Illinois University Press, 1990.

98 "Notes on Young Poets." Allen Ginsberg. Big Table, Issue #4, Spring 1960.

99 The Collected Essays of Robert Creeley. Robert Creeley. Berkeley: University of California Press, 1989.

Philip Lamantia

100 Ekstasis. San Francisco: Auerhahn Press, 1959.

101 Selected Poems: 1943-1966. San Francisco: City Lights Books, 1967.

102   Bed of Sphinxes: New and Selected Poems 1943-1993. San Francisco: City Lights Books, 1997.

103   "Philip Lamantia—S.F. Surrealist Poet." Jesse Hamlin. San Francisco: San Francisco Chronicle, 2005.

104   "Philip Lamantia: Shaman of the Surreal." Thomas Rain Crowe. Milk Magazine, September 1996.

105   "Philip Lamantia: Last Interview." Garrett Caples. Gwynn Oak: Narrow House Recordings, 2001.

106   "Jerusalem." William Blake, 1820.

107   "The Smile." William Blake, 1803.

108   "Holy Sonnet, Batter my heart, three person'd God; for, you." John Donne, 1609.

109   "Psalm 61." David. Revised Standard Version Old Testament, 10th-1st centuries BCE.

110   "Celestial Homework." Allen Ginsberg. www.poetspath.com, 1977.

Gary Snyder

111   Riprap. San Francisco: Origin Press, 1959.

112   Riprap & Cold Mountain Poems. San Francisco: Four Seasons Foundation, 1965.

113   The Real Work: Interviews & Talks, 1964-1979. New York: New Directions, 1980.

114   Paterson, Book I. William Carlos Williams. New York: New Directions, 1946.

115   "Poem as Work-Place: Gary Snyder's Ecological Poetics." Nick Selby. Sycamore 1:4, Winter 1997.

116   The Oxford Companion to Twentieth-Century Poetry in English. Edited by Ian Hamilton. Glyn Maxwell. Oxford: Oxford University Press, 1994.

Philip Whalen

117   Like I Say. New York: Totem/Corinth, 1960.

118   "John Suiter Interviewed by Michael Rothenberg." Big Bridge, 2002.

119   Hagakure, Hidden in Leaves. Yamamoto Tsunetomo,

1716. Hagakure: The Book of the Samurai. Translated by William Wilson. Tokyo: Kodansha International, 1979.

120 Paterson, Book II. William Carlos Williams. New York: New Directions, 1948.

121 Mind Writing Slogans: Allen Ginsberg. Boise: Limberlost Press, 1994.

122 "An Introduction to reading the poetry of Philip Whalen." Tom Devaney. Jacket #11, April 2000.

Lew Welch

123 Hermit Poems. Bolinas: San Francisco: Four Seasons Foundation, 1965.

124 How I Work as a Poet. Bolinas: Grey Fox Press, 1973.

125 Selected Poems. Bolinas: Grey Fox Press, 1976.

126 Ring of Bone: Collected Poems 1950 – 1971. Bolinas: Grey Fox Press, 1979.

127 Li Po, The Chinese Poet. Li Po, translated by Shigeyoshi Obata. Tokyo: Hokuseido Press, 1935. New York: Paragon Book Reprint Corporation, 1965.

128 Genesis Angels: The Saga of Lew Welch and the Beat Generation. Aram Saroyan. New York: Morrow, 1979.

David Meltzer

129 Ragas. San Francisco: Discovery Books, 1959.

130 Poet w / Jazz 1958. Sierra cd, 2005.

131 David's Copy: The Selected Poems of David Meltzer. Edited by Michael Rothenberg. New York: Penguin Books, 2005.

132 Letter to the author, 2006.

133 "Thirty Years of 'Face': Introduction and Tribute to a Poem by David Meltzer." Karl Young. Big Bridge #11, Volume 3, No. 3, 2005.

134 "Books." Bob Riedel. New York Press, Volume 14, Issue 26, 2006.

135 Tulips & Chimneys. E. E. Cummings. New York: Thomas Seltzer, 1923.

136 "Noted: Dale Smith on David's Copy: The Selected Poems of David Meltzer." David Smith. Bookforum, Dec/Jan 2006.

Bob Kaufman

137 Abomunist Manifesto. San Francisco: City Lights, 1959.

138 Second April. San Francisco: City Lights, 1959.

139 Solitudes Crowded with Loneliness. New York: New Directions, 1965.

140 The Ancient Rain: Poems 1956 – 1978. New York: New Directions, 1981.

141 Beatitude, 1. San Francisco: The Bread and Wine Mission, 1959.

142 Ode to Walt Whitman and Other Poems. Federico Garcia Lorca, translated by Carlos Bauer. San Francisco: City Lights Books, 1988.

143 "Bob Kaufman: The Enigmatic Beat Poet." The Academy of American Poets, 2006.

144 "Bob Kaufman: Jazz Poet of the Streets." Natale Peditto. Cross Cultural Poetics, Summer 1998.

Acknowledgements

This book made it through the blue pencil phase thanks to Laura Fletcher, wife, secret ambassador from this rebel territory to the republic of prose, governed by David S. Wills with accuracy and grace.

Larry Beckett

Permissions

"And the fete continues," in Paroles by Jacques Prévert, translation Lawrence Ferlinghetti. English language translation copyright 1958 by Lawrence Ferlightetti. Reprinted by permission of City Lights Books.

"Sun," in Gasoline by Gregory Corso. Copyright 1958 Gregory Corso. Reprinted by permission of City Lights Books.

"Ring of bone," and "To the Memory of Gertrude Stein and William Carlos Williams" in Ring of Bone: Collected Poems 1950-1971 by Lew Welch. Copyright 1979 by Donald Allen, Literary Executor of the Estate of Lew Welch. Reprinted by permission of City Lights Books.

"There is this distance between me and what I see," in Ekstasis by Philip Lamantia.

"Howl, Part I," in Collected Poems 1947-1997 by Allen Ginsberg.

"Bomb," by Gregory Corso, from The Happy Birthday of Death, copyright ©1960 New Directions Publishing Corporation. Reprinted by permission of New Directions Publishing Corp.

"Saleable Titles," by Gregory Corso, from The Happy Birthday of Death, copyright ©1960 New Directions Publishing Corporation. Reprinted by permission of New Directions Publishing Corp.

"Constantly risking absurdity," by Lawrence Ferlinghetti, from A Coney Island of the Mind, copyright ©1958 by Lawrence Ferlinghetti. Reprinted by permission of New Directions Publishing Corp.

"Away above a harborful," by Lawrence Ferlinghetti, from These Are My Rivers, copyright ©1955 by Lawrence Ferlinghetti. Reprinted by permission of New Directions Publishing Corp.

"Walking Parker Home," by Bob Kaufman, from Solitudes Crowded With Loneliness, copyright ©1965 by Bob Kaufman. Reprinted by permission of New Directions Publishing Corp.

"A Poem for Vipers," in Hotel Wentley Poems by John Weiners. Reprinted by permission of the Estate of John Weiners, with special thanks to Raymond Foye.

"A Night in Tunisia," in Hymns to St Geryon & Other Poems by Michael McClure. Reprinted by permission of Michael McClure.

Philip Whalen, "Sourdough Mountain Lookout" from The Collected Poems of Philip Whalen ©2007. By Philip Whalen. Reprinted by permission of Wesleyan University Press.

"6th Raga," in David's Copy: The Selected Poems David Meltzer by David Meltzer. Reprint permission by David Meltzer.

"18 assorted haiku," in Zen in English Literature & Oriental Classics by R.H. Blyth. Reprint permission by Hokuseido Press/ Welcome Rain Publishers.

"Mid-August at Sourdough Mountain Lookout" in Riprap by Gary Snyder.

"70th Chorus" in Book of Blues by Jack Kerouac. Reprinted by permission of SLL/Sterling Lord Literistic, Inc. Copyright by Stella Kerouac, John Sampas Literary Representative, 1995.

Various haiku from Jack Kerouac's Book of Haikus, Enitharmon Press, 2004. Reprinted by permission of Enitharmon Press.

Also available from Beatdom Books

Zoning, by Spencer Kansa.
978-0-9569525-0-9.

Zoning is travelling without moving.
This mind-bending story revolves
around the intersecting lives of a teen-
age occultist, Astral Boy, and a young,
budding porn star, Skyrise Kid.

'Zoning reads like an urban Celine.'
- William S. Burroughs

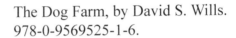

The Dog Farm, by David S. Wills.
978-0-9569525-1-6.

In the 21st century, teaching English
abroad has become virtually a rite of
passage for young university gradu-
ates. In *The Dog Farm*, we see what
happens when this adventure goes
wrong, in a novel about the extremes
of 'culture shock.'

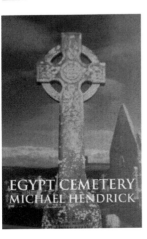

Egypt Cemetery, by Michael
Hendrick. 978-0-9569525-2-3

A somewhat idyllic, sometimes twist-
ed story of childhood in 1960s Ameri-
ca, *Egypt Cemetery* follows the author
from New York's Mohawk Valley and
a nation shattered by JFK's death to
the Cement Belt of Pennsylvania, as
the Beatles arrive at Shea Stadium to
shake up mourning America.

18674562R00088

Made in the USA
San Bernardino, CA
23 January 2015